Countdown 2000

Series editor   *Ziauddin Sardar*

Future Wealth

By the same author

Reform of British Central Government
Profit or People?
Power, Money and Sex
The Sane Alternative
Future Work

Future Wealth

A New Economics for the 21st Century

——— ◆ ———

James Robertson

CASSELL

First published 1989 by **Cassell Publishers Limited**
A book from Mansell Publishing
Artillery House, Artillery Row, London SW1P 1RT, England
125 East 23rd Street, Suite 300, New York 10010, USA

© James Robertson 1990

British Library Cataloguing in Publication Data
Robertson, James, *1928–*
    Future wealth : a new economics for the twenty-first
    century. — (Countdown 2000).
    1. Economics
    I. Title   II. Series
    330
    ISBN 0-304-31930-9
    ISBN 0-304-31933-3 pbk

Typeset by Colset Private Ltd, Singapore
Printed and bound in Great Britain by
Biddles Ltd, Guildford and King's Lynn

Contents

Introduction

"I believe myself to be writing a book on economic theory which will largely revolutionise—not, I suppose, at once but in the course of the next ten years —the way the world thinks about economic problems." Writing to George Bernard Shaw in 1935, John Maynard Keynes overestimated the long-term effect of *The General Theory of Employment, Interest and Money*.[1] As the end of the century comes nearer, the need to revolutionize the way the world thinks about economics and organizes economic life is greater than ever before. We need a new economic order for the 21st century.

This new economic order must be geared to the real needs of people and the Earth. It must be both enabling and conserving. It must restore to the word "wealth" its original meaning of wellbeing. It must harmonize economy with ecology, in accordance with the proper meanings of these words—as the management and the science of our earthly home. It must accept that the era of "the wealth of nations" is past, and treat the 21st-century economy as a multi-level one-world economy.

Transforming the complex of economic behaviour and thought which makes up today's economic order into this new one will be a process of transformation more comprehensive and fundamental than that which Keynes had in mind. It will go beyond economics as economics is conventionally understood. It will go beyond the conventional horizons of capitalism, socialism and the mixed economy. It is, in fact, a process already well begun. It started fifteen or twenty years ago,[2] and its roots go back much further.[3] It has begun to accelerate in the last few years as the urgency for it has become more widely apparent.

During these last few years increasing numbers of people in many countries have been joining together in this endeavour to transform economic life and thought. This book is for them and for the many more who are coming to accept the need for a new 21st-century economic order for people and the Earth, or are open to the idea. When I refer to "we" and "us", I have such people in mind. The book's purpose is to help us to see what we should be aiming to do during the 1990s to hasten and smooth the transition to this new economic order.

This worldwide process of economic transformation cannot, clearly, be completed in ten years' time. It is not the kind of process that can ever be finally completed. We are not engaged in trying to define an ideal economic system, in the hope of eventually being able to achieve it permanently for the rest of time, let alone the hope of bringing a fully fledged Utopia into existence by the Year 2000. We are engaged in changing the direction of economic development and thought, establishing new principles of economic organisation and practice, and stepping up the momentum of change through the 1990s, so that—by the time the Year 2000 arrives—we shall be more or less firmly on course towards a new way of organizing and understanding economic life in the 21st century.

The fourteen chapters of the book fall broadly into five parts.

The first three chapters are about the need for this transformation and its scale and nature, and about getting these more widely understood and acted on in the early 1990s. Chapters 4 to 8 are about the main structural components of the one-world economy—people and their household economies, places and their local economies, national economies, the world economy as a whole, and the organizations operating in these various spheres. Taken together, these chapters outline an evolving structure for the world economy which will reorientate all its component parts towards a more self-reliant and conserving path, and in which a primary function of each larger unit will be to enable the smaller units it contains—e.g. localities within a nation and households within a locality—to be more self-reliant and conserving.

Chapters 9 to 12 are about money, around which so much, though not all, of economic life revolves. They suggest changes in the monetary and financial systems of the world and in our understanding of them, which will make money our servant and not our master. They outline how money could become a fairer and more efficient means for people to conduct transactions with one another in an enabling and conserving economy. They suggest the need to reorientate economic life away from its present emphasis on money, for example as regards what we tax (like incomes) and what we measure (like money-based Gross National Product), towards the real economy, including real resources and the real state of existence of people and the Earth. They point to the probability of a world financial collapse before the end of the century. They compare this reorientation towards real life and away from the abstractions of organized money which is needed now, with the one that took place at the time of the Reformation away from the abstractions of organized religion.

Chapter 13 briefly suggests how the principles of an enabling and conserving one-world economy apply to particular fields of activity or aspects of life. As examples it takes: work; technology and industry; energy; food and agriculture; transport, housing and planning; information and communication; health; education, leisure, and the arts; international peace and security; and science, philosophy and religion.

Finally, Chapter 14 outlines a programme for the 1990s, with key stages in 1992 and 1994/95.

I hope that those who read the book and use it will find it a helpful guide. I hope they will also treat it as provisional. Indeed, I very much hope they will help to make it so, both by their positive actions out in the world and by suggesting to me how it could be made more useful. Ideally, I would like to see it, or at least an expanded final chapter, updated and republished in about 1993 as a guide and stimulus to further progress, and again updated and republished in about 1996.

For those who already know my work, this book builds on past exchanges of information and ideas through the *Turning Point* newsletter,[4] and on my previous books—*Future Work* (1985), *The Sane Alternative* (1978), and their predecessors.[5] It is about creating an economy for person, society and planet—in other words, an economy for the sane, humane, ecological (SHE) future, as opposed to the Hyper-Expansionist (HE) future, discussed in those two books. It particularly reflects my involvement in The Other Economic Summit (TOES) and the New Economics Foundation.[6]

In fact, in the summer of 1986, it was my hope that, following the first three years of TOES and the setting up of the New Economics Foundation, those bodies would be in a position to put in hand the preparation of a new economics strategy for the 1990s. It was a disappointment that it did not happen that way. But, although TOES and the New Economics Foundation should not necessarily be assumed to be behind every idea or proposal that I am putting forward, I very much hope nonetheless that the book will help them and other groups and organizations like them, in other countries as well as Britain, to take forward their indispensable work through the 1990s. I also hope it will encourage people to support them.

Over the years I have been helped in so many ways by so many people, including colleagues in TOES and the New Economics Foundation, that it would be impossible to acknowledge my debt to them all and invidious to thank only a few. Some are named in the course of the book, and many more in *The Sane Alternative* and *Future Work*. But I must again acknowledge my debt to my wife, Alison Pritchard. She has been involved, not just in the writing of this book and reducing some of its faults, but in all the activities that have led up to it—not to mention the stresses and strains that work of this kind sometimes imposes on life at home. I am immeasurably grateful to her.

Notes and References

1. Quoted in Michael Stewart, *Keynes And After*, Penguin, 1967.

2. E.J. Mishan, *The Costs of Economic Growth*, Penguin, 1967, and E.F. Schumacher, *Small Is Beautiful*, Blond and Briggs, 1973, were among those voicing the unease about growthmania which surfaced in the late sixties and early seventies.

3. In Britain they include Ruskin and William Morris in the nineteenth century, and the Distributists in the early twentieth century.

4. The *Turning Point* newsletter was issued twice yearly from 1976 to 1987 by Alison Pritchard and James Robertson (The Old Bakehouse, Cholsey, Oxfordshire OX10 9NU, England) to an international network of people who share a perception that humankind is at a turning point, that old values, old lifestyles, and old systems of society are breaking down, and that new ones must be helped to break through. From September 1989 it is being issued as *Turning Point 2000* with a sharper focus on the 1990s.

5. Details are as follows:

Future Work: Jobs, Self-Employment and Leisure after the Industrial Age, Gower/Temple Smith, 1985.

The Sane Alternative: A Choice of Futures, Robertson (revised edition), 1983.

Power, Money and Sex: Towards a New Social Balance, Marion Boyars, 1976.

Profit or People? The New Social Role of Money, Calder and Boyars, 1974.

Reform of British Central Government, Chatto and Windus/Charles Knight, 1971.

6. Paul Ekins (ed.). *The Living Economy*, Routledge and Kegan Paul, 1986, is based on papers given at the first two TOES meetings in 1984 and 1985. Also see the Appendix.

1

Changing Direction

In the early 1990s we must aim to get it firmly established in the public mind worldwide that the present path of economic development is leading the world to catastrophe, and that this is directly connected with the underlying assumptions and imperatives of conventional economics.

We must get it widely accepted that a change of direction is both necessary and possible, to a new path of economic development for the twenty-first century. The main features of this new development path are discussed in later chapters. In brief:

* it should be systematically enabling for people;
* it should be systematically conserving of resources and environment;
* it should treat the world's economy as a multi-level one-world system, with autonomous but interdependent parts at all levels;
* it should be supported by up-to-date economic ideas.

If this transition to a new economic order for the twenty-first century is to be successfully achieved, the nature of the process—and particularly its links with political change and changes in the structures of power—needs to be widely understood. This is another aspect of what we must aim to do in the early 1990s.

Avoiding Catastrophe

The world's present path of economic development is damaging to both people and the Earth. It is leading the world towards catastrophe. More and more people understand this. An important task for the early 1990s is to make sure that politicians and government policy-makers, business leaders and financiers, professionals and organizational people of all kinds, are not allowed to obscure or forget the following facts.

The 1980s have increased the amount of human poverty and misery in the world, and ecological disaster now threatens. Many people know that today's rates of tropical deforestation, spread of acid rain and other forms of air and water pollution, soil erosion and the advance of deserts, climatic change from the greenhouse effect, depletion of the ozone layer, and mass extinction of species, are unsustainable. By the year 2000, if present trends continue, one third of the world's productive land will have turned to dust, one million species will be extinct, and the world's climate will be irreparably changed. The terrible famines in Africa are just the most striking among many symptoms of the growing sickness of people and the Earth, the devastating long-term effects of which are just beginning to become apparent.

This damage is being done by a world population that is now just over 5 billion. Of these 5 billion people, about a quarter live in the so-called "developed" countries and the other three-quarters in "developing" countries. Per capita, the quarter who live in developed countries consume far more than the three quarters in the developing countries—15 times as much paper, 10 times as much steel, and 12 times as much energy. The consumption of energy by the 750 million people in the richest countries—the industrial market economies of Western Europe, North America and Japan—is actually 17 times as high per capita as that of the 2,500 million people in the lowest income countries. So, even with a stationary world population, if consumption in poor countries were brought up to present rich-country levels this would multiply today's ecological impacts something like ten times over. And world population will not remain stationary. By the Year 2000 it is projected to rise to 6.1 billion and by 2025 to 8.2 billion. Thereafter, it is not expected to stabilize below 10.2 billion on some projections and 14.2 billion on others—twice or three times what it is today. For today's rich-country consumption levels to be achieved by the whole of a world population of that size would mean multiplying today's ecological impacts some twenty or thirty times over.[1]

Anyone who thinks this is remotely possible is living in cloud-cuckoo land. So is anyone who believes that the present polarization of the world's population between a wastefully affluent minority and a very much poorer majority can be indefinitely sustained.

Although awareness that the world is on course to catastrophe has been growing rapidly in recent years, the dominant thrust of conventional economic development offers no solution. Quite the reverse. Modern communications, especially television, are hooking the rising population of the world more and more firmly on the consumerist values propagated by rich-country businesses and governments. This is evident throughout the non-socialist Third World. Even in the socialist economies of the Soviet Union and Eastern Europe—and China too before the terrible events of June 1989—recent economic reforms leave it doubtful whether the switch being attempted is towards a genuinely new path of development or merely to one based on the consumerist example of the market economies of the industrialized West. Meanwhile, as the richest countries have been gearing themselves up to drive still further along the conventional path of economic growth—this being, for example, the stated purpose of the single European market in 1992 and the 1988 Free Trade Treaty between Canada and the USA—the wealth gap grows wider between rich countries and poor, and between rich people and poor people within each country.

A top priority for the early 1990s is to get it firmly established in the public mind worldwide that this whole process is sinfully shortsighted, and that human beings are capable of something better.

An important aspect of this will be to destroy once and for all the notion that economic growth, as conventionally measured and understood, is synonymous with economic and social progress or prerequisite to it. If continued economic growth involves the continued growth of human poverty and dependency, and the continued growth of environmental destruction, then it is bad—unequivocally. If it means technically, as it actually does, the continued growth of the total value of monetary transactions in the economy, then it may or may not be good or bad—depending on who is paying whom how much to do what. But to aim to achieve it for its own sake is, at best, to mistake the shadow for the substance. It was a shame that the Brundtland Commission whose report, *Our Common Future*, contained so much valuable and sensible analysis of the problems now facing humanity, felt it necessary to go along with the call for a new era of economic growth.[2] Its contribution to understanding is consequently much more limited than it might otherwise have been.

A Historic Watershed

Another important task for the early 1990s is to get it understood that these potentially catastrophic developments throughout the world economy stem directly from the basic tendencies and assumptions of conventional economic practice and thought. These basic tendencies and assumptions include:

* the tendency to create and reinforce economic dependency for people, localities and nations;
* the tendency to be wasteful of natural resources and damaging to the natural environment;
* the assumption that economics is about the wealth of nations, and that the paramount unit for economic policy-making must be the nation state.

These key features of the present economic order go back to the 17th and 18th centuries. Modern economic development began with the deliberate creation of dependency, when the common people were pushed off the land, excluded from their subsistence way of life, and made dependent on paid labour. Modern economic thinking had its roots in the perceptions of the English philosophers Bacon and Hobbes—of nature as a limitless resource to be exploited for "the relief of the inconveniences of man's estate", of wealth as power to command other people's labour, and of human life as an incessant competitive struggle for power.

When Adam Smith came to analyse the workings of the economy of his day he followed Bacon's and Hobbes' perceptions of "man" and nature and society. In emphasizing the impersonal role of the market—its invisible hand—and in excluding moral considerations from his analysis of economic life, he was following Newton's example of value-free system-building in the sciences. That Smith also emphasized the wealth of nations, rather than the wealth of people or cities or the world, that he took material production and consumption as the essence of economic life, and that he focused exclusively on activities accompanied by monetary exchange, reflected the most notable economic phenomena of his own time: the struggles between European nations to dominate overseas trade; the astonishing growth of industrial production; and the unprecedented division of labour that accompanied it.

Smith's historical significance was that he articulated a new way of looking at economic life. He thus helped to crystallize a new economic order in place of the vanished medieval economic system which had been conceptually based on the rights and obligations of a divinely sanctioned, static, hierarchical society. That gives a measure of our task today. For the time has come again, as it had in Adam Smith's day, to crystallize a new economic order in place of that which is now failing. The new economic order needed now will be one that reflects the needs and realities of a 21st-century world as far removed from Smith's as his was from the middle ages.

Through the Boredom Barrier

In seeking to steer 21st-century economic development in a new direction, we must recognize an important fact. For many good and sensible people the economy and the "dismal science" of economics have become so abstract and technical, so much the province of supposed experts, and—in a word—so boring, that they have given up trying to make sense of them. The result is that comparatively few people—apart from people with obvious commercial or political axes to grind—have taken a sustained and purposeful interest in the need for fundamental economic change. There have been more comprehensible, rewarding and obviously urgent causes to claim people's support, such as the immediate relief of disaster, poverty and famine, and the conservation of wildlife.

We need to recognize this. But we should not be put off by it. In the last few years, active supporters of many of these more specific, more immediately urgent causes have become aware that today's economic order stands in the way of what they are working for and is at the root of many of the problems they face. It is, after all, the prime cause of ecological disaster, poverty and famine, and the destruction of wildlife.

Growing numbers of social and environmental activists and their supporters and sympathizers now recognize that economics as conventionally understood is not an objective science which must be accepted on its own terms, but an unsound way of thinking that mystifies and distorts both the reality and the morality of people's behaviour towards one another and the natural world. They have learned by experience that economic orthodoxy of whatever variety—capitalist, socialist or a mixture of the two—damages what they care about and systematically obstructs what they are trying to do.

I am thinking of people who support organizations like Oxfam, Christian Aid and the World Development Movement, working to relieve poverty and famine and to help with economic progress in the Third World; like the WorldWide Fund for Nature (WWF), Greenpeace and Friends of the Earth, working to conserve the natural world and the environment; like Schumacher's Intermediate Technology Development Group, working to develop environmentally safe, people-friendly technologies; like the United Nations Association, working to develop effective forms of government for a one-world human community; like the Quakers and other religious groups, working for social and economic justice; like Survival International, working to protect threatened tribal and indigenous peoples in many parts of the world; like the Soil Association and Compassion in World Farming, working for humane and ecologically safe farming methods; and people with countless equally vital concerns in fields such as health, food, poverty, unemployment, housing, education, co-operatives, inner cities, the countryside, the rights of women and ethnic minorities, peace and disarmament, and many more.

Supporters of causes like these and many others, as well as millions of people in their day-to-day lives, find themselves thwarted by the perverse drives and imperatives of conventional economics. They have been learning by experience that, although they are working in a wide variety of different fields and different ways, in one important respect they belong to a single worldwide community of people and organizations, movements and groups. They all share a common interest in changing the practices, policies, assumptions and imperatives of conventional economics.

So another urgent task for the early 1990s is to break through the boredom barrier surrounding economics, and to develop a common framework of understanding and action for change. The aim must be to help many different people, including social and environmental activists and their supporters in many different fields, to see how—without centralized co-ordination—they can reinforce one another's efforts to create a new economic order less damaging to their concerns than the one that now exists.[3]

The Dynamics of Change

The transformation of today's economic order into a new one will be a process of great magnitude and complexity. Another task for the early 1990s will be to generate widespread understanding—not of all the details of this process and all the cross-links between them, which would be beyond any single human mind—but understanding of what sort of a process it will be, what it will involve, what dangers it will throw up, and how these should be dealt with.

To start with, we shall need to recognize that innumerable cross-cutting conflicts of interest and judgement will arise between those who are pressing for change or see the necessity for it, and those who are resisting it or don't. Those who oppose one another on some issues will support one another on others. It will not be necessary for people to pretend they agree with one another on everything, like party politicians subscribing to a manifesto, before they can co-operate with one another on anything.

In support of change there will be both negative and positive factors. In terms of events and happenings, negative factors will include growing evidence of social and environmental degradation and disastrous incidents like Chernobyl, which heighten awareness of the dangers of conventional economic development. Positive factors will include many successful real-life examples of enabling and conserving initiatives, such as self-build housing schemes, poor people's banks, and energy conservation schemes. In terms of ideas, the negative side will include critical exposures of the inadequacies and absurdities of conventional economic practice and thought. The positive side will include ideas that clarify and illuminate the scope for a new enabling and conserving approach, and inspire people to commit themselves to it.

In terms of action, many different kinds of effective action will make their contribution:

* at different levels—personal, local, national and international;
* of different types—through practical initiatives, through political and governmental processes, through the exercise of economic choice, and through information and communication, research and studies, campaigns

and lobbying, conferences and publications, stunts and demonstrations; and

* with different organizational strategies—through existing organizations, by creating new ones, or by working independently of organizations altogether.

One aspect of the complexity of the transformation process lies in the cross-links between these various different forms of action. While it would be impossible to envisage a single co-ordinated campaign embracing them all, we need to recognize how they can all help to reinforce each others' effect on any particular issue.

Another aspect of this complexity is the fact that we now have to understand the world's economy as a single system, consisting of literally billions of subsystems. These include individual persons and households and many different kinds of organizations and enterprises, concerned with all manner of activities, operating at local, national and international levels. Actions by any one of them tend to affect all the others to a greater or lesser extent. But it is not possible to examine them all at the same time. Nor is it very useful to put forward universal conclusions of a general nature—such as that all economic problems could be solved if we all learned to love one another. We have to reconcile the conceptual need to understand the system as a whole with the practical need to change particular aspects of it and to show what particular actions will move things in the right direction.

This means that we have to deal with things in manageable chunks, while at the same time taking account of important cross-linkages between them. For example, changes are needed in policies for local economic development, in the structure and orientation of the energy industries, and in the tax system. Changes in each of these areas have to be considered as a subject in their own right. But the changes required in each can and must also contribute to the changes required in the others.

Other vital cross-linkages are those which link changes in dominant values and beliefs with changes in prevailing theories and models, with changes in what is measured and counted, with changes in objectives and policies, and with changes in organizational structures and procedures. All of these tie in with one another. Changes needed in any one of them will be linked with changes in the others.

Creating Tomorrow out of Today

We also need to understand the central dilemma that faces all who want to create a new future. It arises from the fact that we have to live in, and work with, what exists today. The dilemma particularly affects our attitudes to today's organizations and power structures. If we try to work with them, the risk is that our efforts will be channelled into support for the status quo. If we try to work outside them, or even against them, the risk is that our efforts will be marginalized. A good example is the "green consumer" movement.[4] The running is currently being made by people in industry and commerce and those working closely with them. The danger is that their efforts to promote demand for consumer goods that are environmentally benign will simply result in strengthening the growth of consumerism. Meanwhile, however, those—like the Lifestyle Movement—who support the case for turning away from consumerism altogether, receive no support from industry, commerce or government and have to accept the risk of being marginalized.[5]

People who, while committed to the need for change, are also looking for outer-directed security and success in terms of personal career or wealth or power or publicity, will tend to work with and through existing power structures, whether in politics and government, industry, commerce and finance, the professions, or the information media. They have a necessary role in softening up the established institutions to the need for change. We need to understand its scope and limitations. Others, who may be of a more thoughtful or more rebellious—and perhaps less worldly—cast of mind, will tend to turn their back on the established institutions and work outside them or against them. Their role is necessary, too, and we need to understand its strengths and limitations also.

Working through existing organizations will often be a good way to take forward many of the shorter-term changes in economic practice that will be needed through the 1990s. These are changes that are attainable within the context already generally accepted, on issues that are already on the mainstream agenda. For example, to take the Brundtland Commission again, one way of trying to influence the governmental follow-up to the Commission's Report will be to lobby the governments taking part in the intergovernmental conference being held in Norway in May 1990.

When it comes to longer-term changes, the other approach is necessary. This involves changing accepted ideas of what is possible—creating a new context for decisions by established institutions and bringing new possibilities, now generally dismissed as irrelevant or infeasible, on to the mainstream agenda. Many examples are discussed in later chapters. They include the introduction of local currencies, and the replacement of taxes on income and financial capital by taxes on land and energy and resources. The pursuit of longer-term issues of this kind has to be undertaken outside established organizations, at least up to the point where those organizations can be persuaded or compelled to regard them as credible and worthy of attention. Preaching about the need for these changes to organization people who are simply not ready to be converted, and would be unable to do anything about it if they were, is a waste of time. (Preaching to the already converted can be a waste of time too!)

The Politics of Economic Transformation

That the freedom of creative and innovative action in established institutions is very severely limited, is particularly marked in the sphere of electoral politics. In general, people who belong to a political party find that what they can do and say is limited to the party line, and is dismissed by their opponents and other people as part of the party-political game. When it comes to steps towards a new economic order, existing political institutions and processes are particularly handicapped. They reflect the assumptions and power structures of the old way of economic and political life. They can't avoid distorting the new economic questions of tomorrow to fit the old agenda of yesterday.

Taking British politics as an example, one of the conventional political camps identifies with the interests of employers and owners of capital. It favours the private (or commercial) sector over the public (or governmental) sector. In theory it subscribes to the ideology of the free market, including free trade. In practice, it aims to make people dependent on business and finance rather than on government and trades unions, and supports an international trading and financial system heavily biased in favour of rich nations against poor.

The main opposing political camp identifies with organized employees, and is closely linked to trades unions. It traditionally favours the public against the private sector, and subscribes to the ideology of the beneficent state. Its class base has been declining, and the assumption that governments, whether or not in consultation with trades unions, can have both the will and the capacity to take optimal decisions on behalf of the people, has been losing credibility. Nonetheless, this political approach would still make people dependent on big government and big trades unions, rather than big business and big finance.

In the centre between these two there has been a third conventional political force, split and in disarray at the time of writing. This supports what is known as a mixed economy, in which people will be dependent on a balance of big business, big finance, big trades unions and big government, which will co-operate quite closely with one another in a mild approximation to a corporate state.

The assumption that economic life must be dependent on big economic institutions has been common to all these conventional political approaches, the main difference between them being about the extent to which people should be dependent on business and finance or government and trades unions. Economic policies that will systematically enable people and places to be less dependent on any of these, have simply not fitted into the conventional political agenda. It would be surprising if they had. For the processes and structures of conventional politics have themselves been based on the assumption of institutional dependency. If you want to take part in politics, as politics is conventionally understood, you virtually have to do so under the auspices of one or other of the national political parties, either by becoming a career politician yourself or by becoming a supporter of career politicians. Conventional politics has simply not been about enabling people to be more self-reliant.

The recent rise of green politics has not yet seriously affected this situation. The assumption among the conventional political parties is that they can become as green as they need to be without significant change either to themselves or to prevailing political and governmental processes, simply by adopting environmental policies. Meanwhile, Green Parties—in West Germany, Britain and other countries—have not yet fully come to terms with the possibility that taking part in the game of electoral politics in its present form may be incompatible with the effort to create the new kind of society they want.

This book is not about politics as such, and we cannot take the discussion very much further here. But it is important to recognize that transition to an enabling and conserving economy will have to be accompanied by transition to an enabling and conserving politics. That economic and political transformation cannot be separated from one another has been clearly demonstrated by the events of the last few years in the Soviet Union and China. The Soviet Union discovered that progress with effective reforms on the economic side—perestroika—depended on progress with democratization to break up the log-jam on the political side. China discovered that opening up greater freedom on the economic side created pressures for greater democracy on the political side—which China's rulers, being unwilling to accept, then put down by the unconcealed, unashamed use of violence against their own young people.

The crucial point is that economics is about power. The prevailing structures of economic life reflect prevailing structures of power. The prevailing assumptions of economic theory reflect prevailing assumptions about power. The transformation of today's economic order into a new one for the twenty-first century will involve transforming today's structures of power and today's assumptions about it. This will be apparent in many of the following chapters.

It also prompts the most sobering reflection of all. People with more power and wealth than others do not willingly give them up, and people who enjoy security and order do not willingly see them threatened. It would be foolish to underestimate potential resistance to the necessary economic transformation which we are trying to bring about. It could be disastrous to underestimate the ruthlessness with which this transformation might be suppressed even in law-abiding countries like Britain, if ever it came to be seen as a vehicle for disruptive social and political forces. Whether or not it can be accomplished with the collective political wisdom needed on all sides if it is to succeed, we cannot foretell in advance. All each of us can do is our best to ensure that it is.

Notes and References

1. Statistics in this paragraph are from *Our Common Future—Report of the World Commission on Environment and Development* (the Brundtland Report)—Oxford University Press, 1987.
2. See Note 1.
3. Already, in 1988 and 1989, in association with the New Economics Foundation, a number of British NGOs—Friends of the Earth, Oxfam, Quaker Peace and Service, Survival International, United Nations Associations, World Development Movement, World Wide Fund for Nature—have co-operated in following up the Brundtland Report's recommendations. Information about the resulting publications can be obtained from any of them.
4. References to the green consumer movement are in Chapter 4, Note 4.
5. Information about the Lifestyle Movement is available from Dr John West, 9 Driver Terrace, Silsden, Keighley, West Yorkshire BD20 OJR.

2

Principles

This chapter describes the three key principles for a new economic order geared to creating wealth and wellbeing for people and the Earth. It must be ENABLING (for people) and CONSERVING (for the Earth's resources and environment); and it must be organized and understood as a MULTI-LEVEL ONE-WORLD SYSTEM. An important task for the 1990s will be to clarify these principles and their practical implications.

These are dynamic principles in the sense that they indicate a direction for development and progress. They do not point to a static goal that could be finally achieved. This book is about their application in the next few decades. In a hundred years' time they will still be valid, but the practical ways of applying them will be different from today.

Enabling (for people) and conserving (for resources and environment) are not precisely symmetrical. Enabling people to develop their capacities and potential is more positive than merely conserving what already exists. Enriching the Earth's natural environment and resources would be the counterpart to enabling. The aim of leaving the natural world better when you depart from it than it was when you came in, is certainly a worthy aim for a human life. But, unfortunately, the idea of environmental enrichment as a guiding principle of economic life today seems too far-fetched. For the time being, conserving will have to do. In any case, this conceptual asymmetry is probably not of great practical importance. Environmental conservation shades into environmental enrichment, just as—to take an example of enabling—preventative health care shades into health promotion. Environmental conservation and environmental enrichment both represent environmental investment, just as preventative health care and health promotion both represent social investment. They are all concerned with safeguarding and creating environmental or social wealth.

Enabling

The 21st-century economy must be systematically enabling. Instead of systematically creating and extending dependency, it must systematically foster self-reliance and the capacity for self-development. Self-reliance does not mean self-sufficiency or selfish isolation. It requires the capacity to co-operate freely with others. Self-development includes the development of the capacity for co-operative self-reliance.

Enabling and self-development, as a two-sided process like teaching and learning, should pervade 21st-century economic life. Greater self-reliance, not greater dependence, should be a continuing aim of economic units—persons, cities, nations—at every level of the economic system. Enabling smaller units—such as cities—to become economically more self-reliant and to acquire the capacity to develop themselves, should be one of the main functions of the larger units which contain them—such as nations.

Many of the tasks for the 1990s will involve working out ways of applying the two-sided process of enabling and self-development throughout the world economy, in all its component subunits including the lives of individual people. Examples are discussed in later chapters.

Enabling and self-development will represent a fundamental change from the conventional pattern of economic development. That has created and reinforced dependency and domination. It still does. What is happening in the Third World today repeats what happened in the early stages of development in the industrialized countries one or two centuries ago. First, people are excluded from a self-reliant subsistence way of life and made dependent on paid labour. Then, as development proceeds, dependence widens and deepens. People become conditioned to depend, not only as employees on employers for work. As consumers they become dependent on businesses, professional organizations and government agencies, which then persuade them to regard an ever-expanding range of goods and services as necessities of life.

The dependency created by conventional economic progress applies not only to people, but to countries and cities and other localities too. Many Third World countries today, faced with impossibly large debts, have become hopelessly dependent on the international economy to provide them with export markets and with transfers of technology and finance. Their dependence is paralleled by the dependence of many run-down cities in the industrialized countries, whose national economies are equally unable to revive them.

By developing more self-reliant ways of economic life, and thereby taking more control of their own economic destinies, people and localities will be better able to secure a materially adequate and sustainable standard of living and a socially and psychologically rewarding quality of life—for themselves, for one another, and for succeeding generations.

This will mean more justice and equality in economic life than today, but not the kind of justice and equality that is administered to subordinate people from on high. In the new economic order justice and equality will be brought about by liberating people and localities and nations from dependency, helping them to provide for themselves and one another, and enabling them to take more control of their own economic destinies, rather than by making the less fortunate depend on transfers of welfare and aid from those who are richer and more powerful than themselves.

It is now two hundred years since the French Revolution. An important task for political philosophy during the 1990s will be to reinterpret the roles of liberty, equality and fraternity—freedom, justice and solidarity—in an economic order pervaded by processes of enabling and self-development.

Conserving

The 21st-century economic order must be systematically conserving, instead of systematically wasteful and polluting.

Conventional economic thinking treats material economic activities as if each one were a separate linear process, starting with the extraction of resources (from an infinite pool of resources in the natural world, which is seen as being outside the economic system altogether), continuing with the use of the resources in the production of goods, followed by the consumption of the goods, and ending with the disposal of wastes (into an infinite sink in the natural world, which is again seen as outside the economic system). The result is that today's economic system operates as if it were a machine designed to take resources out of the Earth, convert them into wastes, and return them to the Earth as wastes. By its very nature, it is systematically wasteful and polluting.

The 21st-century economic order, by contrast, must see the whole of economic activity as a single continuing cyclical process, consisting of countless inter-related cyclical sub-processes, with the wastes from each providing resources for others. It must design the economic system as an organic part of the natural world, not as a machine external to it—a reintegration which will also mean giving up the converse assumption that the natural world is a limitless pool and sink external to the economic system. The 21st-century economic system must thus be systematically conserving.

Later chapters discuss examples of what this will mean in specific contexts. The point to emphasize here is that a more conserving approach and a more enabling and self-reliant approach to economic life will be mutually reinforcing. In the first place, using resources efficiently and conservingly contributes to self-reliance. The more a city or other local economy can recycle its own flows of food, water, energy, materials, wastes and money within its own closed-loop system—i.e. the more conserving, as opposed to wasteful and ecologically damaging and polluting, a local economy can become—the more self-reliant it will be. The more it can supply itself with food, energy and materials by using its waste land for food-growing, by capturing energy from internal sources, and by recycling its wastes, the less dependent it will be on imports of food, energy and materials; and the more its people's incomes will circulate within the local economy and generate activity there. As planners are now beginning to see, it makes sense—from the point of view of socio-economic as well as physical planning—to think of a city economy as an ecosystem.[1]

The connection between local economic autonomy and ecological sustainability runs the other way too. Local people who control their own local economy are less likely to waste their resources and pollute their environment than distant decision-makers with no local roots. As the Brundtland Commission found, the integration of economic and ecological goals is "best secured by decentralizing the management of resources upon which local communities depend, and giving these communities an effective say over the use of these resources".[2]

Meanwhile, the World Health Organization's work on Health For All by the Year 2000 has been reaching similar conclusions. WHO's 1986 Charter for Health Promotion stresses "the empowerment of communities, their ownership and control of their own endeavours and destinies" as the heart of the process of strengthening community action on which health promotion ultimately depends; and the concept of the self-reliant, ecological city is providing a focus for WHO's international Healthy Cities programme.[3]

Cities and other localities are not the only economic units to which the ecosystem concept applies. We have to treat households and nations and the global economy itself as ecosystem economies, and work out new approaches to more self-reliant and sustainable development for them. Investing in self-reliance and sustainability will be increasingly relevant to them all.

Social and Environmental Investment

Conventional economic thinking has classified social and environmental measures as wealth consumption, not wealth creation. This has reflected, and been reflected by, the fact that such measures have always been largely remedial. So, health policies and health services have been more concerned with remedying sickness after the event than with positively improving the public health and enabling people to be healthier. And, as the Brundtland Commission put it, "environmental management practices have focused largely upon after-the-fact repair of damage: *re*forestation, *re*claiming desert lands, *re*building urban environments, *re*storing natural habitats, and *re*habilitating wild lands".[4]

The 21st-century economic order will have to reject these conventional perceptions and conventional policy orientations. The idea that economic policies are wealth-creating and social policies wealth-consuming, and that economic policies should therefore be given priority over social policies, is simply not realistic. The world is not like that. This is quite obvious in urban priority areas and other disadvantaged localities, even in industrialized countries. In that context, the need for improved work opportunities, improved housing, an improved health and social environment, improved education, improved leisure facilities, improved incomes and, above all, an improvement in the capacity and confidence of local people to do more for themselves, clearly has to be approached as a single constellation of need—not a collection of distinct and separate needs to be met in distinct and separate ways, some economic and some social.[5] In the context of sustainable development in Third World countries, the Brundtland Commission asked governments to consider abandoning "the false division between 'productive' or 'economic' expenditures and 'social' expenditures. Policy-makers must realize that spending on population activities and on other efforts to raise human potential is crucial to a nation's economic and productive activities."[6]

Investment to create social and environmental wealth will have a vital role in the new 21st-century economic order, and an important strand in 21st-century economics will be to develop the practice and theory of social and environmental investment. New criteria and procedures for evaluating, accounting and auditing such investments will have to be worked out. New institutions will be needed to enable people, as well as public sector agencies, to channel their savings into this kind of investment.

A Multi-Level One-World Economy

The 21st-century economy must be designed and managed as a multi-level one-world economic system, with autonomous but interdependent component parts at all levels.

Adam Smith accepted the assumption of his mercantilist predecessors that national economies were the basic entities for organizing economic life and understanding how it works.[7] His successors, including Keynes and Marx and their followers, continued to take the national economy as the focal economic unit, and the nation state as the principal instrument for measuring, regulating, managing and planning economic activities.

Economic policy-making today is still based on that assumption. On the one hand, national governments insist on controlling the spending of local government authorities as an aspect of national economic management. On the other, international economic relations are based on the idea of sovereign nations negotiating among themselves. Currencies are still issued nationally, not locally or internationally; money is denominated and controlled at the national level. National, not local or international, authorities are still expected to regulate the activities of banks, stock exchanges and other financial institutions.

However, the gap between conventional economic theory and practice on the one hand and economic realities on the other is already growing too wide to be ignored. The need for effective economic policy at the local level is highlighted by the economic problems of cities and rural districts in many parts of the world. Meanwhile, recurring international ecological and economic problems, the increasing need for international economic co-ordination, the growing domination of the world economy by transnational corporations, and the emergence of a one-world financial system based on computer communication between London, Tokyo, New York and other centres, emphasize the need for effective economic policy-making at the global level. To continue to focus on national economic policy-making—whether from a Keynesian, monetarist, socialist or any other standpoint—would simply be to ignore 21st-century realities.

We cannot lay out in advance a detailed blueprint for the emerging multi-level one-world economic system. For example, locality—and therefore the meaning of terms like "local economy" and "local autonomy"—cannot be precisely defined. What people think of as a locality varies from place to place. In population size and geographical area a locality in a remote rural district will differ from a locality in a metropolitan city. Nations differ from one another in these respects too. The Indian Ocean island state of Seychelles has a population of less than 70,000, smaller than thousands of towns and cities throughout the world. The population of China is well over 10,000 times larger. Yet Seychelles has a national economy as China does, together with its own currency, central bank, development bank, annually updated development plan, and so forth. Incidentally, there is no doubt that the people of Seychelles benefit from the control this gives them over their own economic affairs.[8]

But, although we cannot think in terms of a uniformly structured world economy—so many people per household, so many households per neighbourhood, so many neighbourhoods per district, and so on at every level through city (or county), province, nation and continent up to the global level—we must begin to understand the world economy as a multi-level system. We must begin to articulate its autonomous but interdependent sub-economies more coherently than at present. And we must define the principal function of each larger, higher-level economic unit as being to enable its component sub-economies to be more self-reliant and more conserving.

That is the conceptual starting point for advances to be made during the 1990s in many specific spheres. It provides the context in which particular issues, such as the Third World debt crisis or the shape of Europe after 1992, need to be understood. It brings to notice many questions of a practical kind, for example about the scope for local and international equivalents of currencies, central banks, public spending, taxation, and so on. And it provides a useful reminder that systems theory can throw light on the further design and evolution of the world's economic system and its component parts. What all this will mean in particular spheres of economic life, and the practical tasks arising for the 1990s, will be outlined in subsequent chapters.

New Economic Concepts

The key principles of the new economic order discussed in this chapter will have important consequences for theoretical economics. In the light of the new understanding of economic progress which they imply, it will be necessary to re-examine and redefine many economic concepts.

These will include wealth creation and capital accumulation; efficiency and productivity; dependence, interdependence and self-reliance; risk and security; and needs, wants and scarcity. What will be meant by wealth creation, capital accumulation and greater efficiency and productivity for people and organizations operating at each of the various levels of an enabling and conserving one-world economy? And how will they best be measured?

These will be among the kinds of question in our minds as we turn to the need to replace old economic ideas with new.

Notes and References

1. See, for example, papers given by Tjeerd Deelstra and David Morris at the first U.K. Healthy Cities conference in Liverpool in March 1988. The conference proceedings, edited by Dr John Ashton of the Department of Community Medicine, Liverpool University, who organized the conference, are to be published shortly by the Kings Fund, London.
2. *Our Common Future*, Oxford University Press, 1987, p. 63.
3. Helping to draw up the WHO Health Promotion Charter in Ottawa in November 1986 was an exciting and significant event. Information about WHO's programmes on Health Promotion and Healthy Cities can be obtained from the WHO Regional Office for Europe, 8 Scherfigsvej, DK-2100 Copenhagen, Denmark. One of its most notable aspects is the work of Dr Trevor Hancock of the Faculty of Environmental Studies, York University,

Toronto, on the links between public health, the environment and the economy.

4. *Our Common Future*, p. 39.

5. Work which David Cadman and I did for the EEC and OECD in 1985 on finance for local employment initiatives confirmed this.

6. *Our Common Future*, p. 105.

7. Jane Jacobs makes this point strongly in *Cities and the Wealth of Nations*, Pelican, 1986, but argues—mistakenly, in my view—that cities should replace nations as *the* salient entity in economic policy and theory.

8. As desk officer responsible for Seychelles in the Colonial Office in London in the late 1950s, I was involved in drawing up Seychelles' first development plan. Visiting the islands again nearly thirty years later, I could not but be struck by the economic benefits that had come with political independence.

3

New Ideas for Old

An important task for the 1990s will be to spread understanding of the inadequacies of conventional economic thought, and to clarify what can and should be done to remedy them.

Conventional economics is based on primitive conceptual assumptions. It embodies questionable value judgments and incorrect understandings of facts, for example about human nature and the natural world. It reflects what economic life and the state of human development were like two hundred years ago. In short, it suffers from factual error, philosophical misconception, and historical obsolescence. The 21st-century economy needs a stronger conceptual basis than this.

Valuing People and the Earth

The 21st-century economy must recognize the value of people and the Earth.

Conventional economic thinking places no value on people nor on natural resources and the environment except in the context of formal economic activity, that is in the context of earning and spending and of being bought and sold. So, for example, all the rewarding and useful things that people do for themselves and one another in the informal economy, i.e. without being paid—let alone the fact of a person's very existence as a human being—are given no value by conventional economics. And, as we saw in Chapter 2, conventional economics treats the natural world as an infinite pool of resources and an infinite sink for wastes which, being outside the economic system altogether, are deemed to have no value.

Later chapters will discuss ways to rectify this failing of conventional economics. One is in the sphere of monitoring, auditing and accounting where, for example, monetary measurement of national product—as in Gross National Product—is an utterly inadequate indicator of what the economy is doing for people and the Earth. That can only be indicated by non-monetary measurements of human and environmental wellbeing. Another approach, paradoxically, is to develop the use of actual monetary mechanisms, not just notional monetary calculations, to give value to people and the Earth even when they are not engaged in economic transactions. The value of people would be to some extent recognized, for example, by the payment of a basic income to all people unconditionally. And the value of the Earth's resources and the natural environment would be recognized by taxing people who occupy land, extract resources and create waste and pollution.

Beyond Materialism

The 21st-century economy must be understood and designed and managed as an economy in which services, information and culture—and the activities, transactions and relationships which these involve—play a central part, not as if it were still an economy almost exclusively concerned with the production and exchange of material commodities and manufactures.

In the 18th and 19th centuries, economic practice and thought developed around the concepts of supply and demand, production and consumption, as applied to material commodities and manufactures. When, in the 20th century, the provision of services like education and health began to play a greater part in the economy, those concepts were applied to that sphere of activity too; economists and politicians and other public policy-makers and commentators began to think in terms of service "industries". More recently, the application of those same materialist concepts has been extended further, into the spheres of information, communication, scientific research and the arts. Many people are now attempting to understand and organize these as knowledge and culture "industries", revolving around the production, distribution and consumption of "products" such as computer software, television programmes, scientific papers and discoveries, and artistic, musical and dramatic works and performances. Money, too, is something that economists have always tried to understand in material terms, assuming that the supply of money and the velocity of its circulation could be measured and controlled in much the same way as tons of coal or gallons of water.

The growing role of information, communication and culture in economic life, supported by the development of information and communication technologies, now requires us to question this approach. For example, money has now evolved from metal coins, through paper notes and cheques, into electronic messages that debit one account and credit another. Money and finance are now handled as information. They must be understood as information, and the methods for organizing and handling them efficiently and fairly must be designed and managed as information systems. More generally, the production, distribution and use of information—including knowledge, design and skill—is clearly going to pervade the 21st-century economy.

New ways of handling and communicating information can contribute both to the internationalization and to the localization of economic decision-making, in a multilevel one-world economic system. More intelligent use of information, design and knowledge can contribute to a more conserving, less polluting way of economic life. The new information and communication technologies can help to redress the economic imbalance between city and countryside. An information-based economy can be either more enabling or even more dependency-creating than today's. In this respect information and communications technologies are a double-edged sword. They can, if purposefully designed and used, enable people and localities and nations to take greater control of many aspects of their lives and reduce their dependence on organizations and forces outside their own control. But they can also be used to reinforce the dominance of richer over poorer, and of more powerful over weaker, people and localities and nations and cultures. We need to make sure that the first of these two alternatives, not the second, is what actually happens.[1]

Beyond Production and Consumption

Connected with the need to go beyond materialism, the 21st-century economy must be understood and designed and managed as an economy in which activities of value do not necessarily conform to the production/consumption model of conventional economics. Conventional economic thought has considered production and consumption as essentially separate processes, in which the goods and services are produced by some people and then consumed by others.

The idea that production and consumption are necessarily distinct was connected with the masculine model of society prevalent in the 18th and 19th centuries but obsolescent now, in which male breadwinners were expected to go out to a "workplace" in the "world of work", leaving their womenfolk to look after the home and the other "dependants" in the family. The dominant position of men was reflected in the assumption that they were the "economically active" workers who created wealth, whereas other "economically inactive" members of society only consumed it and were a cost and a burden on the economy. Although the economic roles of men and women no longer conform to that stereotype, the concepts that arose from it—such as those in quotation marks in the previous sentence—continue to shape conventional economic thinking. They result, among other things, in the denial of economic value and even economic existence to informal economic activities—as discussed earlier in this chapter.

Conventional economics thus defines production as creating wealth, consumption as using it up, and labour as a cost. Work is seen as activity that people have to be paid to do.[2] Conventional economics attributes benefit to the consumption of products, but not to participation in processes. So, while it can envisage leisure-consumers enjoying leisure-activities provided by leisure-producers, it cannot envisage people drawing positive satisfaction, or getting positive benefit, from actually taking part in productive and useful activities. It cannot envisage win-win situations, in which people positively enjoy activities that help to meet their own needs, or in which they achieve satisfaction or benefit for themselves in helping others to do the same. Thus it puts no value on unpaid voluntary work.[3] Conventional economics can only envisage zero-sum situations, in which benefits of consumption are matched by costs of production.

The centrality of the production/consumption model in conventional economics is directly related to the creation of dependency. The production/consumption model encourages people to think that they cannot do things for themselves, but must necessarily depend as consumers on others—producers—to meet their needs. It encourages them to think of their health in terms of health services and health products for which they must depend on health professionals and a health products industry, and not to create healthier ways of living and healthier living environments for themselves and one another. It encourages them to think of themselves as consumers of information products and artistic products, such as newspapers and television programmes and concerts, and to be dependent on the producers of those products. It does not encourage them to participate more actively in information processes and arts activities.

The 21st-century economy must enable and encourage people to participate, rather than simply produce and consume, and must attribute value to people's capacity to manage their own lives.

Beyond the Impersonality of Capitalism and Socialism

Another of the assumptions underlying conventional economics is that economic activity is necessarily governed by the impersonal mechanisms of either the market or the state, and that it is best understood that way. The theory is that in a pure capitalist economy the market is supreme, with economic activity aiming to maximize monetary profit; that in a pure socialist economy the state is supreme, with economic activity responding to the commands of state planners; and that most actual economies are to some extent mixed, tending towards market or state domination in each particular case.

In practice, capitalist, socialist and mixed economies have all suffered from the same underlying failure—a failure to harmonize personal, organizational and societal goals. The result is a failure to achieve both economic efficiency and social justice, and thus a failure to create wellbeing for all. The failures of capitalism and socialism in this respect have taken recognizably different forms—as have their dominant elites. But in capitalist and socialist economies alike over the past seventy years the pattern of response to these failures has been similar, with the pendulum swinging back and forth as each has tried to solve its problems by going part way towards the other: in capitalist countries from a free market economy towards greater government intervention, and then back again; and in socialist countries from rigidly centralized state planning towards a more market-based economy, and then back again. In spite of these shifts of emphasis, neither the market nor the state nor any mixture between the two has been capable of achieving socially sustainable, let alone environmentally sustainable, progress. Something is missing. A new approach is needed, going beyond both the market and the state.

This new approach will involve recognizing that economic life cannot be successfully organized as if people are different from what they really are. People are not impersonal automatons, governed by the impersonal dictates of market or state. This has its negative aspect. In a capitalist economy the financial and business people who operate the agencies of the market, and in a socialist economy the bureaucrats who operate the agencies of the state, distort their operations in favour of themselves and their associates. Neither capitalism nor socialism, being amoral, offers effective safeguards against institutional corruption of a systemic kind. But the fact that people are not impersonal automatons also has a very important positive side. Since people have a capacity for moral responsibility and choice, they often act altruistically instead of mechanistically following the demands of the market or the state.

Unlike both the capitalist and socialist versions of conventional economics, then, the 21st-century economy must be based on recognition that people are moral beings whose freedom as such should not be narrowly bound by impersonal parameters laid down by market and state. The 21st-century economy must accept, as an aspect of self-reliance, that people need space in which to exercise moral responsibility and choice in their economic lives. Measures designed to allow this free space to people as individuals, and also to groupings of people in local economies and national economies (especially in the Third World), must be part of the new economic order. Possible examples—including, again, the unconditional basic income—are discussed in later chapters.

Beyond Homo Economicus

The new economic order for the 21st century must be based on understanding people's actual nature and needs and motives, and how the economic system itself influences them. To put it another way, our model of the new economic system must be directly related to our model of society and our model of the human being or, as it used to be called, our "model of Man".

Conventional economics avoids serious discussion of people's needs and motivations. It adopts a number of simple assumptions:

* humans are selfish individuals, bent on maximizing their own satisfaction ("utility");
* satisfaction comes from consuming;
* people's needs are expressed in terms of what they are prepared to pay for, and how much ("effective demand");
* people's motives centre on maximizing the monetary value (or notional monetary value) of what they can get from their economic activities.

Twenty-first-century economics must be more sophisticated than that. It must recognize that people have a dual nature. On the one hand, it is a fact that people are prone to greed and self-interest and other human vices. On the other hand, it is also a fact that people are motivated by desire to help and co-operate with one another, and are often prepared to put the common good above their own immediate self-interest. Twenty-first-century economic organization and theory must recognize the dual—selfish and altruistic—nature of human beings, and be designed around it.[4]

This means that the 21st-century economic order must be organized as a system of rights and obligations, risks and rewards, that will:

* channel people's selfishness into the common good;
* prevent people's selfishness from damaging other people's interests, and especially the selfishness of the powerful from exploiting the weak; and
* energize the altruistic desires and capacities of people to help one another as well as themselves, and to contribute to creating a better society and a better world.

Beyond Value-Free Economics

The 21st-century economic order must recognize that economics can never be an objective science that is value-free. Those who say it can are either deceiving themselves or trying to deceive others. It now has to be explicitly recast as what it has always actually been, even in its dependency-creating and ecologically destructive contemporary form—an expression of a political and moral philosophy.

A sense of historical perspective is helpful here.

The transition in the 17th and 18th centuries to today's economic order reflected the rise of new science and the decline of old corrupted morality. Instead of basing their approach to economic affairs on the fading religious and moral insights of the medieval world, new thinkers like Hobbes and Adam Smith based it on what they saw as the actual behaviour of the society in which they lived. Subsequently, the growing emphasis on quantitative measurement in the natural sciences was paralleled by a greatly increased role for monetary exchange and monetary values in economic life. That transition to a new economic order, based on the free market and the national state, was a liberation from old restrictions. It released people's economic energies from moral constraints. It freed them from control by Crown and Church and guilds. It gave economic power to a new cast of actors, unfettered by the old moral and religious restraints.

Today's transition to the next new economic order will also be a liberation from existing limitations, but in a different way. It will release the energies of billions of people now constrained by the requirements of national and international markets and nation states. And this time, by contrast with the previous one, the transition to a new economic order will reflect the rise of a new morality and the decline of a failing scientific approach. One of its key features will be a revival of emphasis on personal and corporate rights and obligations in the economic sphere.

Indeed, rights and obligations must be at the heart of the new economics, as economics becomes re-absorbed in the main body of moral and political thought.[5] This does not mean reverting to a static, hierarchical, God-given economic order such as existed in medieval times. It means developing a human framework of institutions which will enable free people to steer their own economic destinies as they themselves decide, while preventing them from encroaching on the freedom of others to do the same and from damaging the ecosystem on which everyone depends.

In short, the 21st-century economic order must be humanly designed as a system of equal rights and obligations governing the behaviour of free people, their relations with one another, and their relations with the natural world. We must design this system almost as if we were designing a game—in which the rules and scoring system can be clearly understood and fairly administered, in which the balance of risks and rewards encourages people to channel their energies into socially and ecologically positive behaviour, and in which people give one another space to exercise moral choice and moral responsibility. And then we must evolve it into existence by a purposeful stage-by-stage transformation of what exists today.

The rules of this game are laws and the scoring system is money. The rights and obligations embodied in the laws, and the way the laws are administered, should safeguard and enlarge each person's freedom and ability to meet their needs, including their needs for co-operation and self-development, while obliging them to act in ways that safeguard and enlarge the same freedom and ability for other people. And, as outlined in Chapters 9 to 12, the money system too must be designed and operated as a fair and efficient way of regulating and accounting for people's claims and obligations towards one another.

Beyond Smith, Marx and Keynes

This chapter and the previous one have outlined some of the main features of a new economic order and a new economics appropriate to the post-industrial world of the 21st century.

The new economic order must focus on the wealth and well-being of people and the Earth. It must be enabling, not dependency-creating. It must be conserving, not wasteful and environmentally damaging and destructive. It must be concerned, not primarily with "the wealth of nations", but with the operations of the one-world economic system through which the lives of all people on Earth interact with one another and the ecosystem. It must reflect a "model of Man" that recognizes that people have non-material as well as material needs; that these include their need to use and develop their own capacities and potential; and that those include their capacity for co-operation and altruism and their potential as moral beings.

The new economics must thus transcend the materialist assumptions of conventional economics: that economic life is reducible to production and consumption; that wealth is a kind of product that has to be created before it can be consumed; and that wealth production and wealth consumption are successive stages in a linear process which converts resources into waste. It must reinterpret the manipulative concern of conventional economics with the production and distribution of wealth and the allocation of resources, into a developmental concern with how to enable people to meet their needs, develop themselves, and enhance the resources and qualities of the natural world. It must recognize that, because human beings are moral beings, the basic questions about economic life are moral questions. Asking what actually happened in the specific contexts of certain times and places (empirical questions), and what would happen in various imagined situations (hypothetical questions), are useful ways of throwing light on future possibilities. But the questions that matter are about what we are to do. What choices are we to make? How, personally and collectively, are we to conduct and organize our economic lives? And how are we to design and evolve an enabling one-world economic system in harmony with the larger ecosystem of which it is part?

This will amount to a new way of organizing and understanding economic life in which the mainspring of economic progress is no longer the desire and power of people, including organizations and nations, to make other people economically dependent on them. It will mean treating each individual as an autonomous moral actor, interdependent with billions of other persons with equally valid needs, obligations and rights, in a single decentralized world-wide economy. It will mean aligning the economic goals and motivations of organizations and nations with those of people, so that the self-development of each positively enhances the self-development of all.

The period of history now ending is one in which the economic side of human life declared itself independent of other aspects of people's lives and people's relationships with one another and the natural world. As the next chapter shows, this has encouraged and even compelled most people to deal with economic matters without reference to wider social or environmental or moral or philosophical or spiritual considerations. That has been the context in which conventional economic thinking has developed and advanced. And now the economic side of life, and the conventional modes of economic practice and thought, are engulfing everything else and threatening to destroy it. The time has come when economic practice and thought must be reintegrated with other aspects of human and natural life, and made subordinate to human, environmental and moral values.

The key task for the early 1990s is to get this widely accepted in principle, and to begin to make real headway in working out and implementing what it means in practice for economic life and economic thought.

Notes and References

1. The impact of the "information revolution" on economic life and thought is more fully discussed in "The New Economics of Information". This 60-page booklet, containing papers by Tom Stonier, Neville Jayaweera and James Robertson, is available (price £2.50) from the New Economics Foundation, 88–94 Wentworth Street, London E1 7SE.

2. The need to redefine work as an aspect of the transition from the industrial to the post-industrial age, so that its accepted and normal form becomes ownwork instead of employment by an employer, has fundamental implications for every sphere of social and economic life and thought. See *Future Work : Jobs, Self-Employment and Leisure after the Industrial Age*, Gower/Temple Smith, 1985.

3. For a fuller discussion of this point see "The Changing Environment of

Volunteering", the 1987 Geraldine Aves Memorial Lecture—obtainable from The Volunteer Centre, 29 Lower King's Road, Berkhamsted, Herts HP4 2AB.

4. The most notable contribution in this respect so far has been made by Mark A. Lutz and Kenneth Lux in their books *The Challenge of Humanistic Economics*, Benjamin/Cummings, Menlo Park, California, 1979, and *Humanistic Economics: The New Challenge*, Bootstrap, New York, 1988.

5. C.B. MacPherson, in *The Rise and Fall of Economic Justice*, OUP, 1985, and several other books, and John Rawls in *A Theory of Justice*, OUP 1972, are among the political philosophers in recent decades who have given attention to questions concerning economic rights and obligations. A top priority for philosophers of the new economics is now to carry their work forward in the context of an enabling and conserving one-world economy.

4

People

This chapter and the four which follow are about the main structural components of the economic order—the personal and household economy, the local economy, the national economy (and supra-national groupings like the European Community), the global economy, and the organizations (such as business companies) that carry out economic activities. The aim of these chapters, taken together, is to outline the structure of a new economic order that will be enabling and conserving.

We start with people—who are, when it comes to fundamentals, the only economic actors. We are not so much concerned with conventional economic questions about people. These are to do with people in a passive role—as dependents on economic activity—how they should be organized and trained to produce, how they can be given jobs, what they can be persuaded to consume, and what welfare services they should receive. Our agenda is different. It is about how people can be enabled to play a more active part in the twenty-first-century economy. How can people be enabled to become more self-reliant and conserving? What changes in our economic lives will enable us to take more control over them? How can we use our economic power to help to create a more enabling and conserving economy?

These questions apply to human beings everywhere, whoever we are, wherever we live, however we work, whatever kinds of houses we live in, whatever kinds of food we eat. So, although this chapter may seem to apply particularly to people in western industrialized countries like Britain, the same principles hold for people in socialist economies and the Third World.

Some of people's economic activities are in the formal economy. These involve money. They include our activities as paid workers, purchasing consumers, and financial savers. Others take place in the informal economy—in our households and neighbourhoods, where we and our families and our neighbours provide ourselves and one another with useful and necessary goods and services, for most of which no money changes hands.[1]

Conventional economic theory and policy-making assume that, as workers, consumers and savers, we act amorally in pursuit of our own self-interest without regard to wider considerations. Employees are not held legally responsible for their work; their employers are. Consumer advisory services have conventionally limited their advice to "best buys" in terms of value for money. Conventional financial advisers advise savers and investors only about how to get the best financial return for their money. In short, today's economic order operates on the basis that people have no desire and no sense of responsibility to do intrinsically useful and rewarding work, or to use their purchasing power and investing power to make the world a better place.

So far as the household and informal sectors are concerned, the conventional economic wisdom is that these make no contribution of any value to the economy at all. The new economic order must relegate this quirk of the human mind to the realm of historical curiosities, along with the thinking that underlay such questions as how much space is occupied by angels and whether Adam and Eve had navels. Medieval schoolmen and Victorian counter-evolutionists were perfectly serious about those questions. So are professional economists today when they maintain that, if water is brought to Third World households in trucks driven by paid drivers, it makes a contribution to national wealth but that, if it is carried there from wells miles away by unpaid village women on their heads, it has no economic value.[2] And today's economists will seem just as funny to future generations as their medieval and Victorian opposite numbers seem to us today.

This chapter deals, then, with two commonsense facts that the new economic order, unlike today's, must recognize. First, people are moral beings. Their freedom and capability to exercise choice—including moral choice—as employees, consumers and savers must be enlarged. Second, the useful informal activities of the household and neighbourhood can be as good a way of meeting human needs as the activities of the formal, monetarized sector—and in many cases actually a better way. People must be positively enabled and encouraged to participate actively in the informal economy, if they so choose.

Purposeful Workers

The direct way to enlarge people's freedom to choose the kinds of paid work they regard as valuable and to organize it and do it for themselves under their own control, is to alter the conditions in which paid work is done. For example, more open and democratic corporate decision-making in employing organizations will give employees better information about the social and environmental implications of their work, and more say in it. The creation of many more co-operatives and community businesses, the conversion of existing companies and other organizations into these forms, and their acceptance as normal parts of the mainstream economy, will bring wider opportunities for people to work together in pursuit of their own shared aims and values. Making it easier for people to set up their own organizations, and creating the climate and the confidence and the knowhow that will enable people to do this, will be important. Changes like these in the corporate aspects of the economy are discussed in Chapter 8.

The indirect, but perhaps even more important, way to enlarge people's freedom to choose what kinds of paid work they will do, is to strengthen their negotiating position with potential employers. I am not referring here to the strengthening of trades unions, upon which paid workers conventionally depend to represent their interests to employers. I am referring to the need to help people to become less dependent on paid employment altogether. Three ways of doing this stand out, as mutually reinforcing parts of an enabling package. The first is the wider distribution of unearned incomes, for example by providing every citizen with a basic income as of right from the state or the local community, as discussed in Chapter 11. The second, also discussed in Chapter 11, is to distribute capital more widely—not only through wider home ownership and wider share ownership, but also through wider ownership of the physical means of production in the form of land, premises and equipment. The third is to encourage home-based work. This means removing the existing economic and cultural disincentives against home-based self-employment and other kinds of productive work at home, and giving them positive support.

There is a vitally important principle here. The possession of an income, of capital, and of the capacity to work productively in our own homes, can not only enable us to withdraw to some extent from participation in the labour market outside—and so to enlarge the part played in our lives by informal economic activity, as discussed later. By providing us with a degree of independence against people and organizations participating in the labour market who are richer and more powerful than ourselves, it can also enable us to negotiate our own participation in the labour market on fairer and more equal terms. This principle can be applied not only at the personal and household level—which we are discussing in this chapter—but also to local economies and national economies. To the extent that a city can become economically more self-reliant, its people will be able to participate on fairer, more equal terms in the national economy. And to the extent that a Third World nation can become economically more self-reliant, its people will be able to participate on fairer, more equal terms in the international economy.

A vital feature, then, of the 21st-century economy is that it should enable people, cities and other localities, and nations to enjoy a level of economic self-reliance that will enable them to protect themselves from domination by more powerful entities in the larger economic arena outside. This principle should not be confused with conventional "protectionism", meaning the opposite of free trade. Quite the reverse. It is an essential prerequisite for free and fair employment and trading relationships in an efficient market economy.

Purposeful Consumers

Purposeful consumers can exercise their consumer power in at least three different ways.

First, they can boycott products which they see as undesirable, either because of how they are produced (e.g. by sweated labour or inhumane farming), or because of their effect on people (e.g. tobacco and alcohol) or the environment (e.g. CFC-propelled aerosols), or because they come from companies (e.g. Nestle marketing babymilk to the Third World) or nations (e.g. South Africa) whose policies the consumers think are morally wrong.

Second, consumers can positively discriminate in favour of products and services which they wish to encourage for social or environmental or other moral reasons, by buying those products and services in preference to others.

Finally, consumers can reduce their overall level of consumption and buy less. Their purpose in so doing may be to conserve scarce resources, or to leave a larger share of resources for other people, e.g. in the Third World, or to safeguard the environment from pollution. Or it may be to save money, so as to be able to invest it, or give it to charity. Or it may be to reduce their dependence on spending, and therefore also on earning, money—and so to enlarge their freedom to do other things. Or it may be a mixture of some or all of these.

The 21st-century economy must enlarge people's opportunities to exercise consumer choice and consumer power in all these ways.

Again, one of the answers will be better information—from companies and other corporate bodies in their role as producers, as in their role as employers. They must be required to be more open about what their products contain and about the social and environmental impacts involved in their production, use and disposal. If they do not know, or are unwilling to provide, the relevant facts, consumer power should be used to drum them out of business.

Improved consumer advisory services are also needed. Existing consumer advice, such as is provided by the British Consumers' Association and its influential journal *Which?*, should be extended to cover ethical, social and environmental considerations. This is already done by, for example, the Consumers' Association of Penang and in the publications of the International Organization of Consumers' Unions.[3] New consumer advisory bodies specializing in these concerns should also be encouraged. There is already a market for their services in the growing "green consumer" movement.[4]

Retail organizations will have to respond to the growing demands of purposeful consumers. Existing retail organizations are already giving increasing weight to social and environmental concerns, in response to consumer demand. New retail organizations, including producer and consumer co-operatives, should be encouraged to set up with the specific function of providing their customers with socially and environmentally benign products and services.[5]

Measures to encourage conservation, efficiency, and do-it-yourself methods of production will go with the growth of the purposeful consumer movement. These are all ways in which people who want to reduce their total consumption of scarce resources can be helped to do so. People can learn how to use less resources, how to use them more efficiently, how to recycle them, and—both individually and collectively—how to use household and local resources that are at present unused. There is an important role here for new consumer services in the local community.

Purposeful Savers

Just as a wider purposeful consumer movement must be encouraged to grow out of today's "green consumer" movement, so a wider purposeful saving movement must be encouraged to grow out of what is now known as "ethical investment" or "socially responsible investment". Purposeful saving, like purposeful consumption, can be exercised negatively or positively. It can involve refusing to invest one's money in enterprises and purposes to which one is opposed, such as companies producing tobacco or armaments or ecologically damaging products. And it can involve a positive decision to invest in enterprises and projects of kinds which one wishes to support.

How, then, can the new economic order enlarge people's opportunities to exercise moral choice over the use of their savings?

First, better information will again play an important part. Companies and other enterprises seeking investment funds will have to be more open about the social and environmental impacts of their activities.

Second, investment advisory services, like consumer advisory services, must develop an ethical dimension. Existing investment advisory services should extend their advice into the social and environmental impacts of the investments on which they advise. New financial advisory services specializing in these aspects of investment should also be encouraged to set up to meet the growing demand.[6]

Third, banks, unit trusts, building societies and other institutions that borrow or invest people's savings must respond too. Existing investing institutions should be encouraged, by the changing demands of savers, to help people to invest their savings in socially and ecologically benign enterprises and projects. New investment institutions, some of a co-operative character, should be encouraged to specialize in this.[7]

Reviving the Household Economy

The household economy straddles the formal and informal sectors, in the sense that some of its activities bring in money, such as the work of a self-employed person working from home, whereas others do not, such as cooking, looking after the children, mowing the lawn, and so on.

In general, the prevailing assumption today is that the household makes no productive contribution to the economy.[8] What is done at home does not qualify as proper work—"I'm only a housewife"—and while sexist commentators see the housewife as the representative consumer, no one regards her as the representative producer or worker or investor. Home economics is not thought a fit subject for conventional economists, nor household management a fit topic for professors of management. The household is seen as a place for consumption, sleeping and recreation. Even in these non-productive spheres, the replacement of activities within the household by activities outside it is seen as a mark of progress. Conventional economists assume that people who eat in restaurants, sleep in hotels and enjoy leisure activities outside the home are economically more advanced than people who do those things at home.

In pre-industrial times this was not so. The productive lives of men and women centred around their homes. It is only in industrial societies that people have been brought to think that the work of the world is done in workplaces provided by employers and that the economy is "out there". The post-industrial economy must revive the economic importance of the household and enable people to recover control of their own means of production in their own homes. The household must become, and be accepted as, a centre of paid and unpaid work, of learning, of caring, and of conservation—all of which must be recognized as economically important and valuable.

A trend in this direction is already apparent. More self-employed people are working from their homes. So are more employees, including telecommuters linked to their firms by a telephone, a personal computer and an office desk at home.[9] Up-to-date capital equipment in people's kitchens and utility rooms enables people to reduce their dependence on services, like laundries, provided from outside the home. A growing readiness to recycle waste—paper, glass, tins, compost, etc.—is evident. This will turn the household into a centre of conservation, once the facilities become more easily available.

Because this trend runs counter to mainstream economic practices and values, its significance is disputed by those with a vested interest in the continuation of conventional employment as the normal form of work. It needs to be positively encouraged. The need for new ways of distributing incomes and for a wider distribution of capital have already been mentioned. But other measures will be needed to remove the present bias against the household economy, and give it positive support.

These will include changes in:

* planning and building regulations, which now discourage economic activities in people's homes;
* the present tax system which allows firms but not households to charge their costs against tax—(see Chapter 10 on the need to replace taxes on personal incomes and corporate profits by taxes on land, energy, resources and pollution);
* policies on incomes and benefits which now push people into seeking outside paid work and discourage them from unpaid work in their homes (see Chapter 11);
* the present approach to land use, housing and architectural design, which allows little space for productive facilities in and around people's homes;
* the general cultural and educational assumption that activities carried out in the household have less value than the same activities carried out in so-called "workplaces" elsewhere. (A comparable assumption at the national level is that import/export trading is superior to production for the home market.)

These ways of reducing the present bias against the household economy can be supplemented by more positive measures of support for the household in its economic role, matching the types of support provided for business and industry. These could include:

* encouraging research and development (R. and D.) on products, materials, equipments and technologies designed for productive use in the household economy;
* providing more effective incentives and better facilities to encourage conservation and recycling in the household;
* providing management education and training geared to household needs;
* developing and disseminating financial and accounting techniques for the household economy;
* humanizing the "enterprise culture" by recognizing the valuable role played by "lifestyle entrepreneurs"—enterprising people who commit their energies and skills to providing themselves and their families with a

healthy, conserving and humanly satisfying way of life rather than to
routine employment or to financial or career ambition.

Reviving the Informal Economy[10]

In the strict sense of the term, the informal economy covers activities not
involving money, in contrast to the formal economy which covers activities
involving monetary exchange. The distinction is the same as that between:
production for use, directly to meet the needs of the producer or the producer's
family, friends and neighbours, without any payment taking place; and
production for exchange, when a product or service is produced to be sold.
Much of the activity of the household economy falls within this definition of
informal economic activity, but not the money-earning activities of employees
or self-employed people working at home. Much informal activity also takes
place outside the household, for example between neighbours and between
family members living in different households. (A different meaning is
sometimes given to the informal sector as the small enterprise sector, in contrast
to the sector occupied by big business corporations, government agencies,
financial institutions, trades unions and other major players in the national and
international economic leagues. That distinction is directly relevant to the future
of local economies, discussed in Chapter 5. But it is not the distinction we are
concerned with here.)

Economists since Adam Smith have assumed that the informal economy can
be ignored, both theoretically and practically; that "after the division of labour
has once thoroughly taken place" we must all be largely dependent on paid
activities for the necessities of life; and that formal economic activities which can
be measured and counted in money values are the only ones that really matter.
Although economists have recognized that if, for example, a paid housekeeper
becomes the unpaid wife of her employer, her work in the household will not
necessarily become less valuable, they still regard the transfer of activities from
the informal into the formal economy as one of the marks of economic progress.

In laying the foundations for a new, 21st-century economic order, we must
insist that:

* the enlargement of the formal economy at the expense of the informal has
  gone too far, with results that are damaging to both;
* a revival of the informal economy is necessary and possible.

There are three main reasons for reviving the informal economy.

First, informal economic activities can contribute directly to people's general economic wellbeing and to the solution of specific problems, such as unemployment, pressure on social services, and conservation and efficient resource usage.

Second, informal economic activity can liberate people from undue dependence on the institutions of business, government, finance, welfare and the professions, thus enabling them to deal with those institutions from a position of greater strength.

Third, enabling people to undertake informal economic activities, which reduce their dependence on the formal economy, will allow the formal economy to perform its essential tasks more effectively. If business corporations and government agencies and other large organizations are expected to organize work for everyone, provide welfare for everyone, and meet people's every need, they cannot be fully efficient or competitive in their most important function, which is to produce and market the kinds of products and services that only they can provide. If the hospitals, doctors and nurses of the formal health services are expected to administer all the care that everyone needs, they will not be fully efficient at what we really need them for, which is to provide the kinds of treatment and care that they only can provide.

Some of the measures needed to revive the informal economy have already been mentioned—a new approach to the distribution of incomes which reduces people's dependence on paid work, a wider distribution of capital, and support for the household economy. New methods of evaluating informal economic activities will also need to be developed. This is one aspect of the radical reform of existing economic indicators and statistics which is needed to fit them for an enabling and conserving economy.[11]

Men, Women, Children and Older People

The prospective revival of the informal economy and of the household as a centre of economic life raises important questions about the economic roles of men and women.[12]

As the industrial age developed, the split between men's work and women's work widened. Typically, the man became the breadwinner going out to work, while the woman stayed at home unpaid looking after the household and family. The formal economy became the sphere of men, and the informal economy became the sphere of women. In attributing higher status and greater importance to the formal than the informal economy, conventional economic thinking has reflected the corresponding imbalance in status and power between men and women.

For many years women have striven for greater equality of opportunity in the formal economy, with some but by no means yet complete success. But they still shoulder a disproportionate share of responsibility and work in the informal economy. That burden makes it more difficult for them to compete on equal terms with men in the formal economy. The 21st-century economy must be so organized that men and women will share more equally than today the opportunities and responsibilities of both the formal and informal economies. Among the changes that can contribute to this are:

* treating men and women as individual taxpayers on a basis of equality;
* "equal opportunity" measures in the formal economy;
* a basic income scheme (see Chapter 11);
* the revival of the household and informal sectors, as just discussed.

The first two of these will contribute to greater equality in the formal economy. The last two will contribute to greater equality in the informal economy, by encouraging and enabling men as well as women to spend time and energy in productive informal activities.

Today's assumptions about the economic roles of children and old people are also now out of date. In the 21st century it will make no sense to suppose that there is a "working age" of from, say, sixteen to sixty-five containing everyone who is expected to be "economically active", that those on either side of it have no useful contribution to make to the economy, and that therefore they must be regarded as economic dependants. This is particularly obvious at the older end, as increasing numbers of people remain active after retirement. But, as young people's education becomes increasingly intertwined with real-life productive and caring activities, as it should, the same will apply to them too.

In the twenty-first-century economy at least some of the artificial demarcation lines should be removed that now categorize children and older people, together with other people not in employment, as economic dependants. One way of doing this will be to transform today's child benefits and state pensions into basic incomes for children and older people, thereby bringing them into the universal basic income scheme discussed in Chapter 11.

Notes and References

1. The significance of this formal/informal duality in economic life is much more widely appreciated today than it was ten years ago. For fuller discussion see *The Sane Alternative* and *Future Work* and the many references in them to this topic.
2. See Kathleen Newland, *The Sisterhood of Man*, Norton/Worldwatch, 1979, p. 130.
3. In its fortnightly paper *Utusan Consumer* the Consumers' Association of

Penang (87 Cantonment Road, 10250 Penang, Malaysia) regularly includes campaigning items—for example against logging in Sarawak. In *Consumer Currents*—ten issues yearly from IOCU, PO Box 1045, 10830 Penang, Malaysia—the International Organization of Consumers' Unions brings together news items relevant to consumers' interests in the Third World and elsewhere, including many campaigning items relating to social justice and the environment such as the Bhopal gas disaster.

4. In Britain, John Elkington and Julia Hailes brought out their *Green Consumer Guide*, published by Gollancz, to coincide with Green Consumer Week, in September 1988. In 1989 two new consumer magazines have been launched to help readers to use their spending power to create a better world: *New Consumer* (18 Northumberland Ave., Newcastle-upon-Tyne NE3 4XE); and *Ethical Consumer* (ECRA Publishing, 100 Gretney Walk, Moss Side, Manchester M15 5ND).

5. A number of food co-operatives, specializing in wholefoods, have been set up in recent years in Britain and other countries on an explicitly ethical basis. A good local example where I live is called First Fruits. Longer established and better known is Daily Bread in Northampton. The Seikatsu Club in Japan, with over 150,000 households as members and 700 full-time staff, has enough clout—as I heard from one of its managers—to persuade manufacturers of consumer goods to modify their products in accordance with its members' environmental criteria.

6. In Britain the best known example today is Ethical Investment Research and Information Service (EIRIS), 9 Poland Street, London WIV 3DG.

7. British examples that have been in business for some years now include the Ecology Building Society, Mercury Provident Society, and the Stewardship Fund of Friends Provident.

8. There is really no excuse for this any longer. Already in 1975 Scott Burns, *The Household Economy*, Beacon Press, showed convincingly that the household is the strongest and most important economic institution in the USA.

9. Francis Kinsman, *The Telecommuters*, Wiley, 1987.

10. For a fuller discussion, see *The Sane Alternative* and *Future Work*. Also Graeme Shankland, *Wonted Work*, Bootstrap Press, N.Y., 1988.

11. Victor Anderson's book on *Alternative Economic Indicators*, written for the New Economics Foundation, will be published by Routledge in 1990.

12. Also see Sheila Rothwell's contribution on "Flexible Working Patterns" in Paul Ekins, ed., *The Living Economy*, RKP, 1986.

5

Places

This chapter is about the economies of particular places—the local economies of cities, towns, rural districts and villages. How can local economies be enabled to become more self-reliant, less dependent on the national and international economy, and therefore less vulnerable to decisions and events outside their control? How can they become more conserving?[1]

Everyone participates to a greater or lesser degree in a local economy, just as everyone participates to a greater or lesser degree in a household economy. But, until very recently, the role of local economies, like the role of household economies, has been largely ignored by the prevailing economic orthodoxy. Economic policy-makers and theoreticians have relegated localities, like households and families, to the realms of social and environmental policy and theory.

Moreover, just as people and households have become economically dependent on outside employers, suppliers, financial institutions and welfare agencies, so have places. Local economies throughout the industrialized world have become largely dependent on outside employers to organize their work, on outside suppliers to supply their needs (for food, energy, clothing, shelter, entertainment, and so forth), on outside banks, insurance companies and other financial institutions to meet their financial needs, and on outside social service agencies to provide for their health and welfare. Meanwhile, the conventional path of top-down, trickle-down development in the Third World has had the same effect.

For the quarter of a century of sustained economic growth and full employment after the Second World War this may not have seemed to matter very much, at least in a material sense. But in the 1980s the economic vulnerability of many formerly flourishing cities and regions in the industrialized countries became all too apparent. So did the collapse of rural local economies in many Third World countries, leading to famine, or a massive influx of poor people into the cities, or both.

A revival of more self-reliant local economies must be a key feature of the 21st-century world economy. Although this chapter draws mainly on recent experience in industrialized countries, the conclusions apply equally to local development in Third World countries. The material, social and cultural conditions in those countries are very different, and the problems of absolute physical poverty are much more acute and widespread. But the principle of more self-reliant local development, and many practical applications of that principle, are equally valid for people in rich and poor countries alike. To turn any economy which creates local dependency into one that enables self-reliant local development to become the norm, calls for similar changes in psycho-social outlook, economic and financial organization, and political and social power structures.

Although (see Chapter 2) the terms "locality" and "local economy" cannot be at all precisely defined in population size or in geographical area, this need not rule out more self-reliant local development. The same is true of the terms "nation" and "national economy". Iceland and Seychelles are very different from the USA and the Soviet Union. Yet all are nations with national economies. The local economy of a large conurbation will be different in many ways from that of a remote rural area. A local economy will often correspond to a local government administrative unit, such as a city. But smaller areas like villages or neighbourhoods may also be local economies in their own right, if local people think of them as such.

As the importance of enabling and self-reliance as a two-sided principle of economic development becomes established, together with an understanding of the world economy as a multi-level system ranging from the world economy itself to the billions of individual people of whose economic activities it consists, it may be found helpful to think broadly in terms of a hierarchy of local economies (like Chinese boxes within one another)—consisting very roughly of, say, 2,000,000, 200,000, 20,000, 2,000, 200, and 20 households. Any one, or more, of these different levels of subnational economies may, depending on particular circumstances, have some potential for greater self-reliance. For the next few years the practical priority will be to enable more self-reliant local development to proceed in places where it is most clearly needed and where a sense of local identity is strongest. These priority areas will particularly include deprived urban and rural localities where today's economic order has created crisis conditions.

Encouraging Homegrown Local Economies

Until quite recently city governments and other local government authorities, in most industrialized countries with the exception of the USA, had no responsibility for local employment or the local economy; the tasks of local government were primarily social (e.g. education, social services, housing) and environmental (e.g. planning, waste disposal). But in the last few years in most of these countries, with the active encouragement of international bodies like the EEC and OECD, local involvement in local economic policy-making has been developing step by step in response to the problem of local unemployment.

The first reaction of most local authorities to rising local unemployment was to consider how they could attract new outside employers into their locality to replace firms that were withdrawing or closing down. That approach is still being pursued in many places. But, even to conventional economic thinkers, it is now apparent that "smokestack-chasing" and "chip-chasing" mean expensive inducements to incoming employers, who sometimes withdraw from the locality once they have reaped maximum benefit from the incentives they are given; that the best of the new jobs thus created often go to incoming outsiders rather than local residents (as indeed does the best local housing); that incoming firms often continue to use their existing sub-contractors from other localities, thus creating little new local employment; that this approach tends to perpetuate local vulnerability to economic decisions taken elsewhere; and that, even if it does succeed in creating some new jobs, bringing in new outside employers cannot create enough local jobs to solve the locality's problem.

In the last few years, therefore, increasing numbers of localities have begun to encourage the creation of genuinely local initiatives to organize local work to meet local needs with local resources. Many local authorities throughout the industrialized countries have set up investment funds and loan funds, economic development units, and enterprise agencies for this purpose, and have introduced new purchasing policies that favour local enterprises.

A good example has been the Homegrown Economy project in the city of St Paul, Minnesota.[2] Under this project, as described by the Mayor's office, "job creation remains an important goal, but the project broadens the focus by emphasizing the most efficient management of all local resources. Its goal is to extract the maximum value from the community's human, natural and technological resources. Its aggregate results will be significant increases in local wealth, added employment, a more diverse and resilient economic base, increased citizen efficacy, and a self-reliant orientation among St Paul's institutions." In supporting new enterprises, emphasis is given to local ownership, diversifying the local economy, direct benefit to the local community in terms of the products and services offered, and other criteria related to local economic self-reliance. A local fund to provide local venture capital at rates of return lower than the prevailing market rates has been supported by the investment portfolios of a group of local insurance companies—which recognize that they have a direct economic stake in their own local economy—as has a revolving fund to provide loans to businesses that meet the Homegrown Economy criteria.

One aspect of 21st-century economic development must be a systematic approach to local economic development on "homegrown economy" lines. This will involve campaigns and constructive action by local people in all types of local areas—urban, rural, and mixed rural/urban. It will mean working out in each locality:

* ways in which a greater proportion of local needs can be met by local work using local resources;
* ways in which a greater proportion of local income can be encouraged to circulate locally (instead of leaking out of the local economy), in order to generate local work and local economic activity;
* ways in which a greater proportion of local savings of all kinds can be channelled into local investments or loans, in order to contribute to local economic development.

The financial aspects are further discussed later in this chapter and in Chapters 9 to 12. In non-financial terms more self-reliant local economic development will involve many households and many neighbourhoods becoming places where goods and services are produced by the residents for themselves and one another; and in most districts and cities, counties and regions, it will involve a degree of local import substitution, i.e. some replacement by locally produced goods and services of goods and services now coming in from outside. This will affect the production and distribution of food and energy, patterns of industry and employment, the role of education in the local community, planning and housing, and many other aspects of economic life.

Take energy as an example. Increasing numbers of households and organizations will be able to limit and even reduce their dependency on external sources of heat, light and power by adopting modern conservation methods and by supplying some of their own energy needs themselves, e.g. by the use of heat pumps or solar panels. Modern decentralizing energy technologies will enable cities and other local communities to do the same. Possibilities include combined heat and power (CHP); using urban waste as fuel; and—a North American example from a predominantly rural district—paying otherwise unemployed people to cut wood from otherwise unused local woodlots for use as fuel in a small local power station, so reducing both the outflow of local money spent on electricity from a nuclear power station in a neighbouring province, and the cost of paying benefits to unemployed local people.

One need, then, is for in-depth studies of the economics of local decentralization. In the case just mentioned, nuclear engineers and their economists can produce calculations, based on their assumptions of relevance and their criteria of efficiency, to show that local energy production is "uneconomic". But, from the perspective of the local people, using criteria which relate to the efficiency of the local economy considered as a whole, it can equally convincingly be shown that local dependence on external energy sources is uneconomic. It all depends on the perspective. In the 21st-century economy the local perspective must be preferred, or at least given equal weight.

Another need is to identify existing obstacles, prohibitions and discriminations against greater local economic self-reliance, and campaign for their removal. Examples will include planning procedures, and subsidies and incentives of many kinds, which now favour large nationally based organizations against small local enterprises—for example hypermarkets against small local shops.

Investing in Local Self-Reliance

Local economic development requires investment in the locality. Is this to come from outside or from within the locality itself? An integrated approach, involving a combination of the two, is desirable. But each presents a serious problem, which leaves a dilemma to be resolved.

Reliance on outside commercial investment to stimulate local development has an inevitable consequence. The outside investment has to earn a return, in the form of money paid out in future years from the locality to the outside world. This means that regular flows of new money have to be brought into the locality to match the money being paid out, and this requires an increase in exports out of the locality in order to generate the new outside earnings. So new external investment inevitably makes a locality more dependent than it was before on earnings from products and services exported to the outside world—as well as usually increasing its dependence on employment created and controlled from outside. And this is precisely not what self-reliant development is about. To avoid this problem, outside investment in local economic development must be made in a form which requires no new export earnings to service it or pay it back—in other words, external investment must be made either as a gift or grant to the local economy, or as "immigrant" investment in the sense that neither the investment itself nor the earnings from it will subsequently be taken out of the local economy but will be spent and reinvested within it.

The nature of the problem can be seen more clearly if we look at external investment in a Third World country's development. In this case, external loans and investments have to be serviced and repaid in foreign exchange. By their nature, therefore, they cannot be used to reduce the recipient country's dependence on foreign exchange earnings. They have at least to generate the extra foreign exchange needed to service and repay them. The imposition of a necessity of that kind is the reverse of self-reliant development. Self-reliant development involves producing homegrown substitutes for imports, which reduces the need to earn foreign exchange.

In the case of a locality, foreign exchange is not involved. So what is happening is not quite so obvious. But the principle is exactly the same. External commercial investment cannot be used to enable a locality to achieve a significant degree of economic delinking from the larger national economy of which it is part. And that is what more self-reliant local development is about.

However, there is also a problem about a strictly self-reliant approach to local economic development. That would mean relying wholly on locally generated capital for the investment in local productive capacity that is needed to make import substitution possible. But the very places where this approach is most necessary are likely to be those where local capital is least available and where local investment facilities are least developed. The local mobilization of local savings on the required scale may be difficult without outside help.

So there seems to be a dilemma—either investment in dependency-generating development based on export-dependent growth, or no investment in local development at all. How is this to be resolved? It can only be resolved by one form or another of socially directed investment.

Socially directed investment in local self-reliance is investment in the capacities of local people, to enable them to do more for themselves and one another. In other words, it is investment to create local social wealth. Conventional economic investment aims to create a direct financial return for the investor. In socially directed investment, the investor is concerned primarily with non-financial objectives rather than with maximum financial return. The need for new opportunities for people to direct their savings into socially benign enterprises and projects was discussed in Chapter 4. Investment in self-reliant local development is one example of socially valuable investment into which people and organizations might wish to direct their funds, if given the opportunity.

Some of the potential sources of socially directed investment in local economic self-reliance are outside the local economy. Others are within it. Potential external sources include agencies of national government. An example might be a national health department mounting a programme of expenditure on local public health and health promotion that will genuinely enable a locality to become less dependent on nationally supported health services in future years. Potential internal sources include local residents and local organizations, including local government agencies. There are many ways in which they might be prepared to invest some of their money to develop and improve their own locality if the facilities existed for doing so, rather than investing it in ways that mainly benefit other places. And experience shows that poor people, especially in Third World countries, are prepared to save—through credit unions or similar co-operative types of savings institutions—for investment in their own economic future, if they are given opportunities to do so.

An important task for the 1990s is to develop the concepts and practicalities of socially directed investment in local self-reliance, including:

* new priorities for national government spending on local programmes, and
* new financial facilities for channelling local savings into local investment.

The Third Sector

The importance of socially directed investment in local economic development is connected with the fact that the local economy is largely a socio-economy. A third, socio-economic, sector plays a vital part in the local economy, alongside the commercial (or "private") sector and the government (or "public") sector. This third sector consists of large numbers of small enterprises, many of which have mixed social, environmental and economic objectives. (Some people call this the informal sector, in contrast to a formal sector defined as consisting of large commercial and government enterprises and organizations. But it should not be confused with the unpaid activities of the informal economy more strictly defined as in Chapter 4, although it does interlock with them at many points.)

The socio-economic dimension of the local economy cuts across one of the assumptions underlying today's conventional economic thinking—the assumption that there is a clear divide between the economic and social aspects of life. Economic policies and activities are supposed to be concerned with wealth creation, and social policies and activities are supposed to involve wealth consumption. From this it is argued that economic wealth-creating activities must be given priority over social welfare-creating but wealth-consuming activities. From this in turn it is argued that, if the needs of the poor are to be met, the demands of the rich—the "wealth-creators"—must be given priority over them.

An important conceptual task for the 1990s is to unravel the web of metaphysical confusion and mystification that business and financial interests have woven around the notions of wealth creation and wealth consumption. The fact is that the nearer one comes to the realities of actual people's lives, the more artificial the distinction between the economic and social aspects becomes. It is obviously artificial within the household economy. But it is nearly as difficult to sustain it at the local level of the economy, especially in urban priority areas and other disadvantaged localities. As noted in Chapter 2, in such places the need for improved housing, health, education, job prospects, and incomes, and above all an improvement in the capacity and confidence of local people to do more for themselves, is clearly a single constellation of need. It is not a collection of distinct and separate needs to be met in distinct and separate ways, some of them economic and some social.

The practicalities of this comprehensive—or, as some would call it, "holistic"—approach to local economic development were explored at a New Economics Foundation conference on "Converging Local Initiatives" in July 1987. Among our conclusions were that it was becoming increasingly important:

* to provide enabling, rather than dependency-reinforcing, forms of local support and incentives for family care and community initiatives;
* to encourage community architecture, housing associations, health initiatives, information centres, education initiatives, and leisure initiatives—each for their own sake but also as possible starting points for a wider range of grass-roots community initiatives on which local communities can be built;
* to encourage community initiatives in recycling, conservation, city farms, horticulture and energy saving, as steps towards developing more resourceful and conserving communities;
* to enable policy-makers and professionals to help community groups with local projects that cut across sectoral boundaries (employment, health, housing, leisure, etc.);
* to develop techniques of social accounting and social audit in order to measure the benefits produced and the costs saved by community businesses and other local community initiatives;
* to evolve an effective financial and administrative framework for supporting community initiatives;
* to shift the emphasis in public sector social spending from programmes that deliver dependency-reinforcing services to programmes which enable local communities to meet more of their own needs;
* to adapt the structures and procedures of central and local government to their increasingly important functions as enablers of community enterprises and initiatives;
* to expand the role of the voluntary sector, including churches and charities, in local regeneration;
* to enable trades unions to play a positive role in community initiatives;
* to develop management education for community enterprises and

initiatives, recognizing the crucial role of social entrepreneurs whose enterprise is committed not to making money for themselves but to creating social wealth.

Each of these needs is a need for social investment, or—to put it another way—for investment in the local socio-economy.

The Economic Role of Local Government

In the 21st century the role of local government in the local economy should be comparable to that of national government in the national economy. This will contrast with today's situation, where the national government has responsibility for all local economic matters and local government is responsible only for specific functions delegated to it.

The economic role of local government must be to provide a context which will enable local economic activity to be more self-reliant and more conserving. As part of this enabling role, local government should foster more self-reliant household and neighbourhood economies. Just as individual consumers and savers (see Chapter 4) should have more opportunity to channel their money into support of causes they favour, so democratically elected local authorities should be expected to use the collective purchasing power of local people to foster the local economy. It is wrong, as under the Thatcher government in Britain and as proposed for the European single market in 1992, for national and supranational authorities to prevent local authorities from acting thus in the local economic interest if they wish to do so. Indeed, local authorities should be positively encouraged to contract out to local community-based enterprises the delivery of its services to the communities concerned. "Community contracting" of this kind will often be preferable to commercialization (commonly miscalled "privatization") as an alternative to the delivery of local authority services by public service employees.

As part of its local framework, the enabling and conserving economy of the 21st century will need an appropriately designed and coherent system of local taxation, expenditure, and finance. This is one of the topics discussed in Chapters 9 to 12, but the principles on which it should be based include the following:

* local government should not depend heavily on grant-in-aid from the national (or, in the case of the European Community, supranational) government; functions should be distributed between national and local government so as to enable local government authorities on average to raise all the expenditure they need;

* local government authorities should develop new methods of financing their expenditure, by local taxation, local borrowing and other forms of local financing based on new or existing financial institutions;
* the national government should make some redistribution of the national income from richer to poorer localities;
* built into these arrangements should be provisions which provide local economies with a degree of shelter from the full rigours of national (and international) competition and give some encouragement to the meeting of local needs by local work and the use of local resources.

In Chapter 7 I suggest that the third and fourth of these principles should be applied in the international economy too, as a basis for free and fair trading relationships, and for a redistribution of income, between different nations. Study is needed of the feasibility of doing this by levying a uniform international tax on imports and on exchanges of currency—thus discriminating uniformly against import/export transactions—and by distributing the proceeds of this tax to all countries on a per capita basis. But at the local level a uniform, nationally administered import tax—as a basis for free and fair trading relationships, and for redistributing income, between the constituent local economies of a national economy—would hardly be feasible in the absence of local customs barriers.

So what arrangements could provide local economies with a uniform degree of built-in protection against competition from outside, and of built-in discrimination in favour of locally produced goods and services? This is an important question for clarification during the 1990s. Local taxes, local public spending programmes, local banking and local investing agencies, and perhaps even local currencies or quasi-currencies—e.g. for use in local payments to and from the local government authority—may all contribute to the answer, as is suggested in Chapters 9 to 12.

Other Actors in the Local Economy

Meanwhile, there is much that other actors in the local economy can do. Local workers can express a preference for local work. Local consumers can press the companies and shops from whom they buy to employ local people, to prefer local suppliers and generally to make sure that they put as much money into circulation in the local economy as they take out. Local companies and other organizations can voluntarily adopt employment and purchasing policies that have these results, and they can publish information about it. Local savers can seek ways to invest locally. Local volunteers in a whole variety of fields can work and campaign for local resources of all kinds to be used—and conserved—more effectively. Throughout the local economy, social choice in favour of local workers and local products and local services can modify strict financial maximization as the main criterion for economic decisions. The developments outlined in Chapter 4 under the headings "purposeful consumers" and "purposeful savers" will make it easier for local individuals, and therefore also for local organizations, to express their local preferences in this way.

Cities and Countryside

Finally, the accepted relationship between urban and rural economies and their development must be seriously questioned in the 1990s.[3]

Since cities first came into existence they have dominated the countryside and sucked wealth out of it. During the industrial age their economic, as well as political, predominance has grown. Following the industrialized world's example, Third World countries have sought economic progress by favouring urban at the expense of rural development. The resulting displacement of population has helped to create today's urban and rural crises in the Third World, at the same time as the waning of the industrial mass-production economy has created today's urban crisis in the West. The conventional economic approach to city and countryside, to urban and rural development, will have to change. Paradoxical as it may seem, solutions to today's urban problems may depend on a new, more positive approach to development in rural localities, in industrialized no less than Third World countries.

In industrialized countries the economic, social and cultural conditions of "rural idiocy" to which Marx drew attention in the 19th century are now disappearing, as a result of modern technologies and better communication and access to information. It is urban idiocy that is now becoming harder to endure, as cities become less pleasant and less economic places to live in and work in, and as city people become more conscious of their exile from the real world of earth and sky and seasons, and of soil and plants and living creatures, to which human beings belong. And yet financial resources—and therefore physical resources—continue to be channelled into economically unsustainable cities, especially capital cities, to keep the political, professional, managerial, financial and other white-collar elites working there, and to increase the already excessive property values and traffic congestion there. The full economic and social costs of this badly need to be documented.

Documenting them will help to open up a new prospect for the 21st-century. This will be for a greening and villaging of the cities from which the old industrial jobs have gone, and a further shift of population out to country towns and rural areas. More self-reliant, more ecologically conserving, cities will then be able to evolve, accompanied by more diversified development of rural economies, based on manufacturing, services, information and leisure occupations, as well as food production.

For many Third World countries the need for a similar shift in development priorities and for a new urban/rural balance is even more pressing. A viable long-term future for many of today's already over-crowded and rapidly growing Third World cities will largely depend on giving priority to effective rural development, and making it more attractive for people to live in rural areas instead of swamping the cities.

Notes and References

1. My perceptions of what now needs to be done to establish local economies as economies in their own right have been influenced by, among other things: working with David Cadman for the E.E.C. and O.E.C.D. in 1985 on finance for local employment initiatives; organizing a conference for the New Economics Foundation in July 1987 on converging local initiatives (see *New Economics*, Winter 1988); participating in the World Health Organization's recent work on healthy public policies and in the first U.K. Healthy Cities conference in March 1988; and chairing an international working group on rural and urban development at a conference organized by the World Futures Studies Federation and the Chinese government in Beijing in September 1988.

It would be possible to fill several books with notes and references on the various issues discussed in this chapter. So what follows is very selective.

For background, the chapter on "Local Economic Regeneration and Co-operation" in Paul Ekins (ed.), *The Living Economy*, RKP, 1986, and the relevant chapters in Guy Dauncey, *After The Crash*, Greenprint, 1988, are valuable. Ward Morehouse (ed.), *Building Sustainable Communities*, Bootstrap, New York, 1989, deals with specific aspects of "third sector" development. My paper on "The Economics of Local Recovery" for The Other Economic Summit in 1986 (obtainable from New Economics Foundation), my article on "How the Cities Can Finance New Enterprise" in *Lloyds Bank Review*, July 1986, and index references to "local economy" in *Future Work* are also relevant.

2. David Morris, whose *The New City-States*, Institute For Local Self-Reliance, Washington, 1982, stimulated my own thinking at that time, has been playing a major role in the St Paul "homegrown economy" project.

3. David Cadman and Geoffrey Payne (eds.), *The Living City*, Routledge, 1989, based on the proceedings of a conference organized by the New Economics Foundation, is relevant.

6

Nations

This chapter is about economic thinking and policy-making at the national level. Action· at that level has a vital part to play in bringing the new 21st-century economic order into existence. This may seem paradoxical.

Because economic life in the 21st century must no longer be primarily about the wealth of nations, but about wealth and wellbeing for people and the Earth, the adjustment now needed in economic thinking and policy-making at the national level is of key importance. Putting it negatively, conventional macro-economic thinking and conventional national economic policy-making are now the biggest obstacles to the emergence of an enabling and conserving multi-level one-world economy. The challenge is to develop an altogether different approach to economic policy-making and analysis at the national level.

So, although from now on the most important new frontiers for progress in economic action and thought will in many respects be at the household, local and international levels, this does not mean that changes at the national level will be unimportant. Quite the reverse. What it means is that national economies must be reshaped to operate as integral parts of an enabling, self-reliant and conserving, multi-level, one-world economic system in which household and local economies and the global economy are just as important as they are.

In the first place, each nation's economic policies should concentrate on developing a self-reliant, conserving economy for the nation as a whole. Next, each national economy—and all its institutions, regulations and policies—should provide an enabling context for self-reliant and conserving economic development by the nation's localities, organizations, households and citizens. Finally, national economies should be developed as sub-systems of the emerging world economic system; national economic policies should contribute positively to the emergence of a well-functioning and well-regulated world economy.

These three principles are closely related to one another. They apply equally to rich industrialized economies, to poorer Third World economies, and to the socialist economies of countries like the Soviet Union, China, and Eastern Europe. They apply also to such economic entities as the single European market, which the European Community countries are planning to establish in 1992.

Industrialized Countries

How, then, should we set about developing more self-reliant and conserving national economies, less dependent on imports and exports than they now are?

The first step will be to secure acceptance of the basic idea, put forward in Chapter 2, that it is better for sub-systems of the global economic system at every level—national as well as local and household—not to be excessively dependent on economic factors outside their own control nor excessively vulnerable to perturbations elsewhere in the larger economic system to which they belong. This will mean getting it widely understood that a change of direction is now needed from the path of world economic development over the last two hundred years, which has involved an ever-increasing role for imports and exports in most national economies, and has thus led to a disproportionate growth of international trade in relation to world economic activity as a whole. The emphasis must now shift toward meeting a greater proportion of national needs from national work, national production and national resources, with import substitution generally taking priority over export promotion, at least for the foreseeable future. The main exceptions to this will be trade in necessary goods which the importing country cannot for natural physical reasons provide from domestic production, and cultural exchanges including personal travel and tourism.

Many of the policies needed for a self-reliant and conserving national economy will be policies that enable and encourage more self-reliant and conserving development in the informal, household and local sectors of the nation's economy, as outlined in Chapters 4 and 5. But there must also be systematic appraisals of national-level public policy in every sphere to ensure that they foster a more self-reliant and conserving national economy as a whole. These appraisals should cover policies affecting work patterns, technology, industry, agriculture, energy use and many other aspects of economic life, as outlined in Chapter 13.

Changes in present financial arrangements at the national level will be particularly important. As discussed further in Chapters 9 to 12, these should include:

* a systematic redesign of the tax system to shift the burden of tax on to activities that use resources or are environmentally wasteful, polluting or

damaging, and away from useful work and activities that are socially and environmentally benign;
* a systematic review of public spending programmes to shift spending away from programmes that encourage or reinforce dependency or are environmentally wasteful, polluting or damaging, and into programmes that encourage and enable people to meet their own and one another's needs or are socially or environmentally benign in other ways;
* reforms of the national and governmental accounts, to distinguish more clearly than at present between capital and revenue transactions, and to show changes for the better and for the worse in the economic, social and environmental state of the nation;
* reforms in the annual budgeting and forward planning procedures for government revenues and expenditures, so that the options for decision can be more clearly and openly presented to parliament and the public;
* changes in the structure and regulation of the national monetary and financial system, to make it operate more efficiently and openly as a system for allocating resources according to personal and collective needs and choices.

As back-up to all these changes, and to the campaigning and lobbying and public debate required to press them home, studies and research will be needed to show how a more self-reliant, enabling and conserving national economy might be expected to develop over the years. Much of this research should explore hypothetical scenarios. For example, what changes would have to take place and be likely to take place in the British economy as a whole (or whatever other national economy is under consideration):

* if the country were to become more self-sufficient year by year in food, timber, energy and all manufactured goods, reaching—say—85 per cent self-sufficiency in the year 2000?
* if repair, reconditioning, reuse and recycling (the 4 Rs) were to become as important as manufacturing (in terms of value added) to the national economy by the year 2000?[1]
* if an unconditional basic income scheme were phased in over the ten-year period starting in 1995?
* if the present disparities of incomes and wealth between poor people and rich people were to be reduced by some specified amount by the year 2000?

Many such future possibilities should now be carefully specified for research and study in depth, so that the practical implications of moving towards a more self-reliant, enabling and conserving national economy can be better understood, and so that feasible targets for progress in that direction can be adopted.

So far as their external economic relations are concerned, national governments should be pressed to avoid unilateral protectionism. This tends to be damaging nationally, as well as internationally, except in the very short run. International trade should be regulated by international arrangements designed to foster self-reliant national economies by giving all countries an equal level of protection against foreign imports. All countries will thus enjoy space in which to develop more self-reliant national economies, and—while being required to respect one another's space—be enabled to trade and invest with one another freely on equal terms in fair competition. This need for a new model of international free trade, appropriate to the one-world economy of the 21st century, is discussed further in Chapter 7.

Third World Economies[2]

The peoples of many Third World countries have been becoming poorer in recent years. The countries of sub-Saharan Africa are obvious examples, but per capita incomes have also declined during the 1980s in many other countries, including Argentina, Philippines, Peru, Mexico and Brazil. For many Asian, African and Latin American countries, military conflicts and the continuing diversion of scarce resources to weaponry and military manpower, stimulated by the interventions of superpower geopolitics and the international arms trade, have not helped. But quite apart from that, the forecasts for many of the poorer countries are that, for the next ten years or so, economic growth rates will not exceed population growth.

Economic prospects in the industrialized world offer little hope for the conventional development approach in these poorer countries. Governments in the leading industrial countries claim that the 1980s have been an economic success story. But, if that is so, it has not provided the engine of growth for world economic development which, according to conventional economic thinking, would have enabled the economies of the poorer countries to develop satisfactorily. The steps now necessary to deal with the United States trade and budget imbalances, doubts over the future of the dollar as the world's main trading currency, the repercussions of these factors on other industrialized economies and their effects on the international stock markets and currency markets, the emergence of trading blocs based on the United States, Western Europe and Japan, and the broader implications of these developments for the world economy as a whole, will not help in this respect. Hope triumphs over experience and common sense in the minds of any who genuinely and sincerely expect the industrialized countries to provide the conventional engine of export-led growth for the countries of the South, at least for the next ten years. In the normal course of events, the industrialized countries quite clearly cannot be relied upon to provide the expanded markets or the increased financial transfers that would be needed for this.

That is an objective assessment of the situation as it exists today. If, as we are suggesting must happen, the industrial countries reduce their own dependence on imports and exports and move towards greater local and national self-reliance, the consequent effect on the international economy will make it all the more unrealistic for Third World countries to rely on export-led growth as their main development strategy, and all the more necessary for them too to concentrate on local and national economic self-reliance.

These external arguments reinforce the very strong internal ones in favour of a shift of emphasis towards self-reliant Third-World-country development. This should involve three major shifts of priority:

* investing in the productive capacities of people rather than simply in physical production technologies;
* investing in the development and conservation of natural resources and the environment;
* investing in reduced dependence on industrialized countries and the world economy for technological innovation, food imports and financial transfers.

These three shifts in priority are closely related. They parallel the comparable shifts of priority now needed in industrialized countries.

Investing in the Capacities of Third World People

Human investment is more important than physical investment. The productivity of new technologies depends on the skills, intelligence, confidence, stamina and experience of the people who are going to use them. The capacity of those people to stimulate the further technological, agricultural and industrial innovation needed in local conditions is crucial for self-sustaining further development.

More specifically, the need to invest in women and children as centrally important agents of development must now be recognized and acted upon, together with the need to cushion the particular vulnerability of women and children to economic recession and the "adjustments" conventionally required by the International Monetary Fund .

Development for women, with women, by women, must be a central feature of development strategies in many countries from now on. In sub-Saharan Africa, for example, women form three quarters of the agricultural labour force, and are almost wholly responsible for household provisioning; yet their role in the food system has been largely ignored hitherto, and sometimes actually made more burdensome, by conventional agricultural research and innovation. The case for giving higher priority to productive innovation in food-growing systems and household provisioning systems, in contrast to the conventional focus on male agricultural activities, is overwhelming. This will require special arrangements for recruiting many more women into agricultural research and extension services, for establishing women's rights to land, and for enabling women to have access to credit—as has been done successfully already in certain places.[3]

High birth rates and rates of population growth are closely related to family poverty; and large family size is, in turn, a cause of poverty. It is women, again, who play the crucial role here, as well as more generally in household health and in bringing up children—the vital factor in future productivity and development. Giving higher priority to primary health care and to intersectoral programmes for community health promotion, as encouraged by WHO's Health For All strategy, will bring big economic pay-offs in later years as well as immediate benefits for the women and children (and men) directly involved in these programmes. A similar re-orientation of priorities in education and technology will be needed to provide future farmers and other rural workers with the skills, equipment and competence they will need to develop the rural economy, rather than providing them with an escape route from the rural sector into the already overcrowded towns and cities. In all these linked fields—food-growing, household provisioning, health, education and appropriate technology—future strategy must enable the people of the communities concerned to play a major part in defining, with professional help, the innovations and developments they want.

Investing in the Environmental Resources of the Third World

The damage done to future development prospects by failure to invest in people, and especially in the well-being of women and children, is matched by the damage caused by failure to invest in the conservation of natural resources and the environment. The threat of environmental bankruptcy is infinitely more alarming than any threat of national financial bankruptcy could ever be.

The droughts and floods and deforestations of the 1970s and 1980s in Africa and Asia and Latin America have exposed the vulnerability of the food production systems and methods of land use which conventional development has encouraged. Everywhere economic pressures—no less than demographic pressures—have led to the "mining" of land and other resources. An important aspect of resource management for the future will be the establishment of land rights, water rights and forest rights for local communities, so that—quite apart from securing the survival of the peasant and tribal and forest peoples themselves— they will recover the incentive and responsibility to conserve land, water and trees for their own future use. If cutting firewood brings an immediate income while planting trees or refraining from cutting them confers no right to any future return, the continuing destruction of trees is virtually assured.

So far as the continuing destruction of the rainforests on a national and multinational scale is concerned, the whole world is now aware of the dangers that this is creating for us all. The international action needed to enable countries like Brazil and Indonesia, and other Third World countries, and even regions like the Arctic, to break through to an ecologically sustainable path of development—not based on quarrying their natural resources for export—is discussed in the following section of this chapter.

The agriculture of Third World peoples, their use of resources and the conservation of their environment cannot be directed successfully by transnational corporations based elsewhere, by government development agencies in capital cities, or by scientists in conventional agricultural research institutions, but only by the people who have the biggest and most direct stake in them. From now on, successful development will have to be based on a multitude of small schemes for enabling local farmers, local businesspeople, and their families to work and live more productively and more conservingly, not on a comparatively small number of big plantations, big dams, big factories and other prestige projects.

Investing in Economic Self-Reliance for the Third World

We have seen that the poorer countries of the South will be very misguided if they try to rely on export-led growth in the coming years. The measures they now take to meet emergency needs, to stabilize decline, and to rehabilitate eroded economic capacity, should give preference to building up internal self-reliance rather than to increasing exports. Measures designed to reduce the spending of foreign exchange will be preferable—other things being equal—to measures designed to increase the earning of foreign exchange. The right strategies closely resemble those outlined in Chapter 5 for the more self-reliant development of local economies. Third World countries should rely as much as possible on domestic savings rather than on external investment capital, and they should encourage production and consumption patterns which minimize the use of foreign exchange.

Internally, this will entail many changes, such as the following:

* new patterns of co-operative self-reliance, embodied in new productive associations between the primary agents of development—that is men, women and children in their own local communities;
* new rights and responsibilities of local communities in respect of the natural resources on which their future depends;
* new enabling relationships between professional people (agricultural, medical, technical, etc.) and the people for whom and with whom they are working;
* new forms of intersectoral co-operation on local developments in agriculture, health, education, industry, technology, etc.;
* a new emphasis on rural, as contrasted with urban, development;
* new less dominant and more enabling relationships between governments and people; and
* a new enabling role for transnational corporations.

The parallels with the approach to local economic development outlined in Chapter 5 will be very clear.

Externally, attempts by Third World countries to de-link—at least to some extent—from the international economy, and especially from economic dependence on industrialized countries, face two problems. The first is how to pay off—or write off—existing debt. The second is how to acquire the imported technologies and skills which even a development strategy aiming at internal economic self-reliance will need. As described in Chapter 5, it is one thing to borrow external capital for investments that will generate foreign exchange earnings to service the debt so incurred. It is quite another to borrow it for investments designed to make foreign exchange earnings unnecessary. How, in the latter case, is the debt to be serviced?

It is sometimes suggested that Japan might be willing, even eager, to invest Japanese trade surpluses in a "new Marshall Plan" for the Third World, instead of in other industrialized countries including the United States. There would indeed be a nice paradox here: Japan, whose export-led growth strategy has been such a resounding success, helping less successful countries to reorientate their economies toward a strategy of import substitution and economic self-reliance. There would also be an interesting symmetry. Japan, of all countries, now faces a compelling need to reorientate a growing proportion of its own productive capacity away from exports towards internal domestic consumption. However, paradox and symmetry will not be enough to solve the same old problem. If Japanese trade surpluses are invested in self-reliant internal development in Third World countries rather than in production for export, how—without earning any additional foreign exchange—will the recipient countries be able to service and repay or otherwise provide a return on these investments? Is it suggested that all this Japanese investment should take the form of free gifts and grants?

There is no escaping the truth, much as rich-country banks and governments have tried. Somehow, the Third World countries must secure a significant easing of their present debt burden and a once-for-all injection of financial and technical aid as a gift from the rich countries. The aim should be to enable these Third World economies to achieve internal stabilization and to generate the momentum needed for self-reliant development by the Year 2000. They would then be in a position to decide, according to the internal and external conditions existing at that time, whether to try to get back to the old conventional path of export-led growth and so "re-link" with the industrialized-country economies in something like their present relationship to them, or to continue on a path of local and national economic self-reliance, or to adopt whatever mix of the two seems likely to suit them best.

There are strong arguments, of both equity and self-interest, why the rich countries should now ease the burden of Third World debt and invest a further once-for-all gift of financial capital and technical aid in self-reliant, ecological Third World development.

In developing their own economies in the 19th and early 20th centuries, Britain and the other industrialized countries of the West enjoyed much more favourable circumstances for development than most Third World countries do today. As increasing agricultural productivity drove people off the land, and as—in the early stages of industrialization—birth rates rose and death rates fell, there was room for the surplus population of Britain and other such countries to migrate not only to the cities of their own country but also to many other parts of the world. Moreover, there were then no ecological constraints on industrialization. No-one ever demanded that early industrial Britain should stop cutting down its forests and polluting the air. No-one had heard of the ozone layer or the greenhouse effect. No-one worried that uncontrolled development in 19th-century industrializing Britain might damage people elsewhere in the world. Finally and perhaps most telling, many of today's industrialized countries—as dominant trading powers in the 17th and 18th centuries—drew capital for their own subsequent development from the profits of exploitative foreign trade, including the slave trade, with the countries of Africa, Asia, the Pacific and the Americas; and later, as colonial powers, they continued to draw capital from, and exploit tied markets in, many of those countries. This historical debt remains to be repaid by the industrialized to the less developed countries.

Self-interest argues strongly that the peoples of the rich countries should now repay this debt. Unless we can find an effective way to help the billions of people in the poorer countries of the world to break through to self-reliant, conserving, sustainable forms of development in the next decade, the whole world will face ecological and economic breakdown. The peoples of the rich countries must compel their leaders to understand this and act upon it in the 1990s.

This whole question of Third World development is closely bound up with questions about the future regulation of international trade and aid and finance, including international taxation. These are discussed in Chapter 7.

The Soviet, Chinese and Other Socialist Economies

The unprecedented changes now taking place in the Soviet Union and the countries of Eastern Europe will clearly help to shape the 21st-century economic order. Future economic developments in China will have just as powerful an impact in the long run. But at present it is hard to see precisely how what is happening in the socialist economies will affect the prospects for an enabling and conserving world economy.

At first sight, the changes that have been taking place in the socialist economies in recent years seem to have consisted largely of attempts to liberate the market forces and consumerist forces associated with the capitalist West. Chinese television, at least until the latest upheaval, has been given over to advertising consumer goods, and millionaires have been asking to join the Chinese Communist Party. In the Soviet Union private enterpreneurs are building up fortunes under the guise of "co-operatives". As Gorbachev put it in "Perestroika': "the essence of what we plan to do throughout the country is to replace predominantly administrative methods by predominantly economic methods.'[4] And the Chinese leadership was talking of a move to a "socialist commodity economy", a phrase in which "commodity economy" more clearly signified a shift in favour of market forces than "socialist" signified how market forces were to be qualified.[5]

However, both the Soviet and Chinese leaderships have been adamant that they are not simply reverting to capitalism. As Gorbachev put it, again in "Perestroika": "We aim to strengthen socialism, not replace it with a different system. What is offered to us from the West, from a different economy, is unacceptable to us. We are sure that if we really put into effect the potential of socialism, if we adhere to its basic principles, if we take fully into consideration human interests and use the benefits of a planned economy, socialism can achieve much more than capitalism."[6] The Chinese leadership was insisting similarly that the "concept of socialist commodity economy is a breakthrough in the economic theory of Marxism, a development of theory and practice in scientific socialism".[7]

So, although the socialist economies have so far seemed even less open than Western industrialized or Third World economies to the idea of a 21st-century economic order based on enabling and conserving, this may reflect their particular circumstances at the present time—and also, perhaps, our lack of close contact with their thinking. That socialist-country leaders insist that their economies are not simply falling into line with the prevailing economic orthodoxies of the West is important. At the very least it means that influential actors in the world economy are looking for something new. But we do need to strengthen contact with people in the socialist countries, wherever this is possible, to learn how much potential support there is there for the kind of new enabling and conserving economic order we are proposing.

There is certainly support for some aspects of it. One of the things Gorbachev said in his important speech to the United Nations in New York in December 1988 was that "the world's economy is becoming a single organism, and no state, whatever its social system or economic status, can develop normally outside it." That is not very far removed from the idea of a multi-level one-world economy. The need for environmental conservation is now very widely accepted, though not yet very effectively acted on, in the socialist economies. There is a lot of potential scope for co-operation on new economic thinking there. The emphasis we place on the need and scope for the exercise of economic responsibility and power at the personal level, and for enlarging the economic role of the household sector and the informal sector, may present difficulties for socialist ideology—as it does for died-in-the-wool capitalists. But this just emphasizes that a priority for the 1990s will be, whenever possible, to identify sympathetic non-governmental organizations to work with in the socialist countries, of the types which—both in the West and in the Third World—have been making the running in this field.[8]

The Single European Market, 1992

The twelve member countries of the European Community aim to achieve a single market by 1992. This will involve removing all obstacles to the free movement of goods and services, capital and labour between member countries, and harmonizing their regulations and tax systems to provide fair trading conditions across their national boundaries. Progress towards achieving this in 1992 is gathering momentum.

Some of the issues raised by Europe 1992 concern future developments in the world economy. Those will be dealt with in the next chapter. Here we are concerned mainly with the issues which Europe 1992 raises for the national economies involved.

The stated purpose of the single European market is the expansion of conventional economic growth. The main emphasis—at least so far—is on creating a Europe for businessmen, from whom all good things are supposed to originate. Environmental and social considerations are regarded as subordinate.

As yet there has been no serious suggestion by European governments that Europe 1992 should be used as an opportunity to enable the people and communities of Europe to take more control over their economic lives or as an opportunity to create for the people of western Europe an economic way of life that would be more conserving of natural resources and the environment. As yet there has been no suggestion from European governments that this consolidation of a European-level economic entity should be accompanied by the emergence and recognition of more self-reliant economic entities at the subnational level too. The main disputes so far have been about the possibility that the new Europe might be dominated by multi-national bureaucrats instead of multi-national businessmen, and about the extent to which national economic functions should be transferred to Brussels: should national currencies, for example, be replaced by a single European currency, and national central banks by a single European central bank?

Our main task for the 1990s is not to obstruct the emergence of a more unified economic entity at the European level. It is to help to shape its development into something different from what is now proposed.[9] Looking outwards, the European Community should evolve into a continent-level component of the 21st-century multi-level one-world economy. Looking inwards, it should evolve into a framework that will encourage the nations and localities within it to develop more enabling and conserving economies of their own. What this means in practical detail, and how it is to be brought about, are questions on which a great deal of work is needed. Two examples are the following.

By the first decade or two of the 21st century, most of the economic functions traditionally carried out by nation states will have their counterpart at the European level. These include public expenditure and taxation, together with currency management and the other functions of a central bank. However, this need not and should not mean that these functions cease to be carried out at the national level. We should envisage their being carried out at all levels—global, continental, national and local. Indeed, they should be designed that way as a means of articulating the autonomous but interdependent functioning of the multi-level one-world economy's component parts. Study and discussion will be needed through the 1990s of how the functions of taxation, public expenditure, currency and central banking will best be dovetailed with one another at European, national and local levels—and at the global level also.

The second question specifically concerns public expenditure. I touched on it in Chapter 5. After 1992, according to existing proposals, public purchasing will be thrown open to "fair competition" on a Europe-wide basis. "Fair competition" is interpreted as meaning that national and local government agencies in the member countries will be prohibited from using their purchasing power—i.e. money belonging to the people of their own nation or locality—to favour suppliers from their own nation or locality, even if this clearly contributes to the wellbeing of the national or local economy. The same prohibition will not apply to the purchasing decisions of business organizations, however large. Given the public service functions of government and the profit-making functions of business, this is clearly perverse.

There is, of course, a problem. If all national and local government agencies had carte blanche to use their purchasing power in favour of suppliers from their own nation and locality, this could result in rapidly spreading protectionism—and even favouritism and corruption. Effective democratic control over public spending will help to avoid that danger. But it may also be desirable to build into the European economy a uniform differential in favour of local suppliers and national suppliers, when they tender for contracts from local and national purchasers. This would make it easier for local and national suppliers to compete for public contracts in their own locality or nation, while establishing uniformly fair conditions of competition throughout Europe between businesses in different localities and different nations. An approach to this question was suggested in Chapter 5, in the context of local economies. The same point is discussed in the next chapter, in the context of international free trade.

In the next two or three years up to 1992 there will be increasing public debate in all the European countries about the impending single European market, and especially about its social and environmental implications. It will be important to use this opportunity:

* to mount a programme of research and discussion on what an enabling and conserving European economy for the 21st century will look like, and what should be done to bring it into existence;
* to build strong working links with non-governmental organizations and groups in other European countries that share the same aim;
* to establish regular contact with those people working in the institutions of the European Community and other European institutions who are sympathetic towards the local, social and environmental aspirations of the peoples of Europe.

As 1992 approaches, and then as the first results of the single European market begin to make themselves felt in the years between 1992 and 1995, there is likely to be a rising tide of protest and an increasingly widespread and powerful backlash against the whole idea of a multi-national businessman's Europe which is socially damaging and environmentally destructive. It will be important to be ready by, say, 1993 with a well-worked out and well supported scheme for transforming the European Community—through the rest of the 1990s—into an enabling and conserving framework for the national and local economies of Europe.

Notes and References

1. John Davis has powerfully argued that the substitution of the 4Rs (repair, reconditioning, reuse and recycling) for a proportion of manufacture must be an essential part of a new direction of economic development. See, for example, John Davis and Alan Bollard, *As Though People Mattered: A Prospect For Britain*, Intermediate Technology Publications, 1986.

2. This and the following sections of this chapter originated in a set of papers on "New Modes of Co-operation: How and Why" by The Other Economic Summit on prospects for development in Sub-Saharan Africa, which I presented to an international symposium held in Geneva in 1987 by the Association Mondiale de Prospective Sociale (AMPS). The symposium, attended largely by francophone Africans, was organized and chaired by Professor Albert Tevoedjre —the then Secretary-General of AMPS, who is now President of the Pan-African Social Prospects Centre in Porto Novo, Benin.

I should also mention two Institute of Development Studies papers by Robert Chambers which I have found particularly illuminating—No. 227 of December 1986 on "Normal Professionalism, New Paradigms and Development", and No. 240 of December 1987 on "Sustainable Livelihoods, Environment and Development: Putting poor rural people first". And, of course, the Brundt-land Commission's report—*Our Common Future*, OUP, 1987—is essential background.

3. A good example is the SEWA Bank (Self-Employed Women's Association, SEWA Reception Centre, opposite Victoria Garden, Ahmedabad, India). Women's World Banking (684 Park Avenue, New York, NY 10021) provides international banking support for women's grass-roots banks like the SEWA Bank.

4. Mikhail Gorbachev, *Perestroika: New Thinking for Our Country and the World*, Harper and Row, 1987, p. 88.

5. Prof. Tong Dalin, Vice-Chairman and Secretary-General of the Chinese Society for Research on Restructuring the Economic System, explained this approach in a paper on "Reform, Opening, and the Movement to Emancipate the Mind in China", which I heard him give at a conference in Beijing in September 1988. The title of his paper is ironic, after the events of June 1989.

6. Mikhail Gorbachev, ibid. p. 86.

7. Prof. Tong Dalin, ibid.

8. In 1989 the New Economics Foundation made valuable contacts with Soviet economists Vladimir Kollontai and Mikhail Lemeshev.

9. In 1989 the New Economics Foundation initiated work on the new economics implications of the European Single Market. The *"New European" Quarterly Review* (14/16 Carroun Road, Vauxhall, London SW8 1JT) always contains valuable, thought-provoking articles.

7

The World Economy

In recent years the world economy has devastated the lives of millions of innocent people, it has been transferring resources systematically from poor countries to rich countries, and it is destroying the Earth. It is disabling and ecologically destructive. How can we turn it around and make it enabling and conserving?

The first problem is that the workings of the world economy are made to seem so complicated that most people give up trying to understand them. This suits many of the international bankers, businesspeople, officials, politicians and economists most closely involved. Having served their apprenticeship in this rewarding field, and having been associated with what has been happening in it, they have a vested interest in keeping it to themselves.

It is therefore a top priority for us to:

* clarify in our own minds how we think the world's economic institutions should work and how they now need to be reformed, and mount a worldwide campaign of public discussion about it;
* find ways to persuade the experts to say how they think the world economy should now develop, in words people can understand;
* recognize nonetheless that what many of the experts have to say, imprisoned as they are in governmental, financial, business and academic institutions, each with their own self-regarding agendas and specialist spheres of expertise based on the past, may be less constructive than the sustained exercise of our own common sense and common morality.

The key point is that the world economy has now become a single economic system. What happens in one part of the world increasingly affects what happens in others. Raising interest rates in rich countries raises the cost of Third World debts, so increasing the transfer of resources to rich countries from poor countries, aggravating the poverty of poor people in poor countries, and pressurising them to use up and damage their natural resources and environment. The acid rain caused by power stations in Britain kills trees in Scandinavia. People eating hamburgers in the North causes tropical forests in the South to be cut down for cattle ranching. Destruction of tropical forests causes global climate change. In countless such ways as these, the economic responsibility of people in one part of the world for what happens to people in others is growing all the time.

The long-term task, therefore, is:

* to design international rules and institutions and practices which will reflect the reality of a one-world economy, and which will systematically encourage enabling and conserving ways of economic life in every part of the world; and
* to evolve these rules and institutions and practices over the coming years out of what exists today.

The resulting new structure of international economic organization should foster a sustainable but developing world economy: enabling, not dependency-creating as today; socially just, not biased towards towards the richer and stronger countries as today; and conserving, not wasteful, polluting and destructive of natural resources as today.

A Multi-Polar Economic World: Two Scenarios

Recent and current developments in the world economy create the context in which we must tackle this task.

In the past two centuries, the workings of the world economy have reflected and reinforced the dominant economic position of one nation. In the 19th century it was Britain, and the principal international currency was sterling. Since the mid-20th century it has been the United States, and the principal international currency has been the U.S. dollar. As each of these two nations in its time dominated world trade and finance through its relative supremacy in industrial and financial affairs, its currency became acceptable to other governments as a medium in which to hold their financial reserves, and to other countries' businesses and governments as a medium of international exchange. As each of these two nations thus became world banker, it benefited, as the USA still benefits today, from the real resources transferred to it from other countries in exchange for its currency. This is one of the many features of today's international economy that systematically transfers resources from poorer to richer countries.

This era of single nation predominance is now coming to an end. As American economic hegemony wanes, no successor nation is in sight. Japan, the European Community, the Soviet Union, China, India—none of these seems likely to take the place of the United States as world economic leader. Nor is single nation predominance giving way to bi-polarity. World economic dominance is not going to be shared between the United States and the Soviet Union, as they have shared world military dominance for the past few decades. As the 21st century approaches, the world economy is moving into a more pluralistic, more genuinely international phase.

How will this work out? There are two main possibilities. We can think of them as Oligarchy and Democracy.

Oligarchy is a scenario in which the world economy develops into, and is managed by negotiation between, a small number of powerful trading blocs. Though the precise details are not important at this stage of the discussion, the blocs would be on something like the following lines.

> *West European*: European Community, with special links to some resource-rich former colonies.
> *American*: United States, Canada, Mexico, Central America and Caribbean, with special links to certain other countries like Korea, Taiwan and Israel.
> *Japanese*: Japan, ASEAN (Indonesia, Malaysia, Philippines, Singapore and Thailand), Australia and New Zealand.
> *Russian*: Soviet Union, East European members of COMECON, and possibly India.
> *The Rest*: China, Latin America, and the rest of the Third World.

The Oligarchy scenario now seems in some respects more probable and in some respects less probable than it did a few years ago. The single European market planned for 1992 and the recent U.S./Canada free trade agreement look like steps towards it. Developments in the Soviet and Chinese economies and their opening to the outside world—at least, in the case of China, up to June 1989—seem to point in the other direction.

The Democracy scenario, which is the one we favour, does not ignore the undoubted tendencies towards these larger trading blocs. But, as outlined in Chapter 6 with reference to the European Community, it requires them to be prevented from becoming inward-looking and protectionist, which would merely result in the richer peoples of the world continuing to rig the conditions of trade against the rest. It envisages the emergence of these supranational areas within which conditions of free and fair trade have been established as one of the possible steps towards a more fairly and efficiently organized one-world economy.

For that to be so, however, it will be necessary—as the Democracy scenario envisages—for there to be further developments in international economic institutions. Those now existing were set up at Bretton Woods after the Second World War. They now need to develop the whole range of functions—wider and more closely articulated than today—which, in an enabling and conserving one-world economy, will need to be carried out at the global level. These functions include taxation and public expenditure, currency management and the other functions of a world central bank, and the regulation of international finance, business activity and trade.

World Taxation and Public Expenditure

The functions which taxation should be designed to perform at the global level are the same as at other levels: to raise the revenue needed for public expenditure; to encourage economic self-reliance, useful enterprise, and the conservation and efficient use of natural resources, and to discourage and penalize waste, pollution, nuisance and crime; and to redistribute financial resources from rich to poor.

The amount that needs to be raised by taxes at the world level will depend on how world public expenditure develops (see below). With that in mind, research and discussion is needed on the detailed feasibility of various possible taxes, including:

* international taxes on activities that exploit international resources, such as ocean fishing and sea-bed mining;
* international taxes on activities that pollute and damage the global environment, or that cause hazards across national boundaries, such as destruction of the ozone layer, acid rain, dumping of wastes at sea, and nuclear power;
* a uniform international tax on imports between one nation and another;
* a uniform international tax on international currency exchanges, that is exchanges between one national currency and another, or between national currencies and a world currency.

Whether a single market, such as the European Community after 1992, should be treated as a nation for any or all of these purposes, is one of the questions that will have to be agreed between it (and its member nations) on the one hand and the rest of the world community on the other.

The last two of these proposals—for international taxes on imports and currency exchanges—have been mentioned already. They embody the principle that all economic entities should be enabled to enjoy a degree of insulation against domination by external economic forces and against external economic perturbations over which they themselves can have no control. The case for some such buffering or insulating mechanism to provide national economies with an agreed level of protection, within a world trading system that could then be much freer than today's, was strongly argued by Keith V. Roberts in his privately and posthumously published *A Design for a Market Economy*.[1] Roberts suggested that the whole of the present worldwide system of domestic tariffs and international trade restrictions might be replaced by a single international tax on imports. He suggested a 20 per cent tax, together with an international duty of 1 per cent on all international currency transactions. But he stressed that those figures were given only as a basis for discussion. "The tax would be paid by the importer to an international body, such as the IMF or the World Bank, and the total receipts would then be credited to the account of member governments in proportion to their national populations. This would automatically provide aid to the Third World at a level of between 3 per cent and 4 per cent of the total world income."

Roberts based his proposal for such a buffering mechanism on systems theory. As he put it, "To use a mechanical or electrical analogy, coupled sub-systems are most stable when the coupling is rather weak. When the degree of coupling exceeds a certain level, the whole system can become violently unstable". If completely free international trade were ever to be realized—which in practice it never has been and never will be—it would almost certainly create a violently unstable world economy. The world trading and financial system should be designed to buffer its component parts from the dangers of such instability, and otherwise to leave them free to compete with one another on fair and equal terms in export markets. If, as a bonus, the best way to do this provides international tax revenues for redistribution in favour of poorer nations, so much the better.

As Chapter 4 pointed out, the same principle can be applied to individual people through a Basic Income Scheme. An unconditional basic income will provide people with space, within which they will enjoy a degree of protection from the full rigours of economic competition, and outside which it will therefore be possible for a much freer labour market system to operate than today's. The need for a comparable arrangement for giving local economies space, within which they can enjoy a degree of insulation from the competitive rigours of the national economy, was mentioned in Chapter 5.

Future developments in world public expenditure will depend on how the functions of the United Nations and the whole range of its associated global agencies, such as the World Health Organization, Food And Agriculture Organization, UNESCO, and so on, develop in the 21st century. This is too large a question to go into here. As the 50th birthday of the United Nations in 1995 draws nearer, interest should begin to focus on the prospects for its second fifty years and for the further evolution of the functions of international government at the global level. For that reason—and others—we may expect discussion to intensify within the next few years about the U.N.'s role in the first half of the 21st century, and about providing the expenditure to support its expanding activities.

Over the longer term an increasing proportion of U.N. and associated expenditure seems likely to be financed by regular sources of international tax revenue. A World Tax Authority will probably be needed to administer these. Some of the revenue—e.g. from international imports and currency exchange taxes—may be used, as suggested above, to finance transfer payments to poorer countries as an automatic, unconditional form of what is now called "aid". Some of it—e.g. from taxes on international resources and pollution—may be used to finance the international inspectorates needed to monitor the depletion of international resources and other aspects of the international environment. These are among the matters now urgently needing research and debate. New methods of financing international governmental expenditure at the global level, e.g. by the U.N. and its agencies, will undoubtedly be a significant feature of the 21st-century one-world economy.

A World Currency

The U.S. dollar is now the world's main international currency. It is used for international trading and financial transactions. International loans are mostly made in dollars. Countries hold their financial reserves in dollars. But this will not continue for very much longer. There are technical reasons for this, connected with the continuing U.S. trade and budget deficits. But underlying these is the more basic fact that the United States no longer dominates the world economy as it did after the second world war and as Britain did in the 19th century.

Theoretically, it might perhaps now be possible for a multi-currency form of world financial and monetary management to evolve as an aspect of the Oligarchy scenario. International monetary holdings and transactions are now computerized, and exchanges between one currency and another can now be effected almost automatically, using up-to-the-minute calculations of their relative values. This might make it feasible for several leading currencies—e.g. ecu, dollar, yen, rouble—jointly to perform the functions of international trading and reserve currencies, at least for a time. This is a possibility that could usefully be explored. But I believe that what is needed is a new world currency, to be introduced as one of a wider package of reforms in the international financial and monetary system.

This being so, a key task for the 1990s is to study and discuss the feasibility of a genuine world currency, to be used in parallel with national (and continental) and local currencies. It should probably be based on a "basket" of major national currencies, much as the ecu (the European currency unit) is based on a basket of European Community member currencies. It should probably be issued, much as Keynes originally proposed at Bretton Woods in 1944, in the form of credits to national governments. In the first instance it should probably be issued to the governments of poorer countries as part of a package of measures for eliminating their debts and investing in their self-reliant development, as proposed in Chapter 6. It should probably be issued by a new world monetary authority (or world "central bank"). This might be evolved out of the International Monetary Fund and the Bank for International Settlements. One of its main jobs will be to manage and supervise the use of this new currency in the international economy.

These possibilities should be urgently studied and debated. They are among the changes now needed in the international financial and monetary system to bring up to date the arrangements which were agreed at the Bretton Woods conference in 1944 and introduced in 1945 after the Second World War.

International Trade[2]

What role will be played by international trade in an enabling and conserving world economy? We need to go beyond the old arguments about free trade and protectionism, and it is important to get the principles clear.

We should start by recognizing that the world has never had a genuinely free and fair trading system. Ever since people argued whether trade follows the flag or the flag follows trade, trade has been based on domination and dependency, and has been an instrument of them. The ideology of free trade has been used, as ideologies often are, to justify the strong in taking advantage of the weak and to persuade the weak that it is neither conceptually respectable nor in their own best long-term interest to protect themselves.

Today's international trading arrangements are as powerfully biased as ever against the interests of poorer countries. Textiles and clothes are one of the areas in which the hollowness of rich-country rhetoric about free trade can be clearly seen. When the interests of their own producers are adversely affected, in this and other spheres of manufacturing, the rich countries settle for protectionist policies. Free trade principles and the legitimate interest of Third World producers take second place.

An even clearer example is food and agriculture.[3] World farming subsidies averaged $246 billion a year in the three years 1984 to 1986. The chief offenders are the richest countries. The chief sufferers are the poorest countries. Between 1980 and 1986, farm subsidies rose from 15 per cent to 35 per cent of farmers' income in the USA, from 36 per cent to 49 per cent in the EEC, and from 54 per cent to 75 per cent in Japan. The resulting reduction in food imports into those countries, and the resulting increase in the export of food surpluses from them at low prices, have reduced export markets for agricultural products from many Third World countries and—even worse—have seriously damaged their rural economies by reducing incentives for domestic food production.

A real danger in the coming years is that protectionist policies will become stronger in the three trading blocs crystallizing round the USA, Europe and Japan. Such policies might not only lead to trade wars between those blocs themselves. They would also be very damaging to the poorer countries of the Third World, insofar as these were still trying to export to the industrialized world or were still being required to do so in order to pay off their debts.

As a basis for a new international trading regime in the 21st century, we need to start from the following principles and explore their implications and their feasibility.

* The total volume of international trade—as a proportion of total world economic activity—should fall, as nations and localities everywhere move towards greater economic self-reliance and more conserving economies.
* This reduction in the volume of international trade should not be brought about by national governments (or trading blocs) unilaterally introducing tariffs and subsidies and quotas, i.e. by old-fashioned protectionist measures, which distort the internal working of their own economies as well as distorting the conditions of international trade.
* It should be brought about by developing a new international regulatory framework for trade—including such measures as the international imports and currency exchange taxes discussed above—which will affect all countries uniformly, and which will encourage greater self-reliance and a more conserving use of resources, while also providing a basis for free and fair international trade where necessary.

The main point is that, from now on, the evolution of the world's trading system must be linked with the concept of self-reliant, sustainable development. More specifically, it should be closely tied in with resolving the present Third World debt problem, with the introduction of international taxation and a new systematically redistributive approach to aid, with the further development of the international monetary system and the Bretton Woods institutions including the IMF and the World Bank, and with the future regulation of international business and finance.

GATT (General Agreement on Tariffs and Trade) and UNCTAD (United Nations Conference on Trade, Aid and Development) should probably now develop into a fully fledged International Trade Organization (ITO), of the kind originally proposed in 1944. ITO should probably also take over responsibility for regulating the activities of transnational corporations (see below). ITO would then take its place, alongside the new World Tax Authority and a new-model IMF, in a tripartite arrangement for regulating international trade, taxation and finance. These possibilities need urgent study and debate. How the present World Bank and other UN development programmes and agencies will fit into the new arrangements are among the questions that need to be researched, discussed and resolved.

The IMF and the World Bank

The International Monetary Fund (IMF) and the World Bank (International Bank for Reconstruction and Development) came into existence on 27th December 1945, following the Bretton Woods conference in 1944. Their 50th anniversary is due in 1994/5.

Even when they were set up, the functions defined for them reflected the problems of the past, at least to some extent. The IMF, in particular, was charged with ensuring that in the post-war world the obstacles which had bedevilled international trading relations between the industrialized countries in the 1930s—unilateral tariffs and quotas, competitive devaluations, lack of convertibility, and other impediments to foreign exchange transactions and international capital flows—did not arise again. The IMF's purpose was to foster an international trading and financial environment of the kind thought likely to suit its two main architects, Britain and the USA. Its terms of reference committed it—and still do—to promote the expansion of international trade, and to eliminate foreign exchange restrictions which hamper world trade.

Forty years on in the 1980s, the IMF has found itself dealing largely with the problems of countries which were not very much in mind when it was set up—the "developing" countries. The IMF was not intended to foster development and still disclaims any direct concern with it. But the conditions it lays down when national governments seek its help in dealing with balance-of-payments difficulties, do in fact impose on the countries concerned a development strategy based on export-led growth. For the Third World countries caught up in the debt crisis of the past decade this has meant a development strategy which locks them into deeper dependence on the industrialized countries and compels them to mine their long-term environmental resources to meet their short-term need for foreign exchange.

The effects of the IMF's ideological orientation towards the expansion of international trade has thus had a damaging impact on Third World development. It has been quite the reverse of enabling and conserving. In practice, its ideology has led it to adopt policies geared first to the interests of bankers, politicians and bureaucrats in the rich and powerful countries, second to the interests of a rich and powerful minority in the poorer countries, and not at all to the interests of the majority of people in poor countries.[4]

The World Bank was originally set up to foster reconstruction and development in the post-war world. So, unlike the IMF, it is at least supposed to be concerned with development. But its approach to development, like the IMF's, has turned out to be disabling and environmentally destructive. The kind of development it has fostered has made the developing countries even more dependent on the industrialized world and on their own traditional economic role as exporters of primary commodities, raw materials and resources. The Bank's agricultural policies have—no doubt to some extent inadvertently—led to the further impoverishment of poor farmers and have made many of them landless. The Bank's urban housing projects have led to the further impoverishment of poor slum dwellers and have made many of them homeless. Many of the big development projects the Bank has supported in countries like Indonesia, the Philippines and Brazil have had a devastating effect on the livelihoods of tribal peoples, leading in some cases to their near extinction. Industrialized forestry projects and big dams and irrigation schemes have made a few rich people in Third World countries even richer, but many poor people even poorer. In practice, the World Bank's policies have turned out to be geared to the interests of bankers, industrialists, engineers, bureaucrats and politicians, and hardly at all to the interests of the majority of people in the Third World.[5]

The underlying reason for the World Bank's now obvious failure to have fostered the kind of development needed by most of the people in Third World countries has been suggested in earlier chapters. External investments of loan and equity capital require to be serviced and eventually repaid in foreign exchange, which can only be earned by increasing exports. Investments of that kind simply cannot lead to self-reliant development. They are bound to lead to deepening economic dependency.

In short, as the 50th anniversary of the IMF and World Bank approaches, their functions and operations (together with those of other U.N. development agencies and programmes) need to be fundamentally overhauled and re-orientated. Only then will they be able to play their part in an enabling and conserving one-world economy for the 21st century.

Transnational Corporations

Transnational corporations (TNCs) play a key role in the international economy. The 56 largest TNCs have annual sales ranging from $10 billion to $100 billion. TNCs are responsible for a very large proportion of international trade. For example, trade associated with TNCs represents between 80 per cent and 90 per cent of the exports of both Britain and the USA.[6] TNCs loom large in international capital flows, and are responsible for the bulk of foreign direct investment and international transfer of technologies. By internalizing international market transactions within themselves they can by-pass many of the controls exercised by national governments. Their bargaining power allows them to negotiate with many governments from a position of strength and to play one country off against another, for example over inward investment decisions. In countries which cannot stand up to them, they can sell products and enforce working conditions which are unacceptable elsewhere. Whether we like it or not, they are here to stay—at least for the foreseeable future.

How, then, can TNCs be encouraged to play an enabling and conserving role in the world economy, and how are they to be controlled?

TNCs can be encouraged to play an enabling and conserving role, as all other companies can, by bringing market forces to bear on them within the countries where they operate—for example through people adopting the purposeful approach to work and consumption and investment suggested in Chapter 4, and through the kinds of changes in the tax system suggested in Chapter 10.

So far as control is concerned, the shift to new institutions and procedures for a one-world economy, as outlined earlier in this chapter, will provide the context needed for more effective international regulation of TNCs. Part of the problem today is that even the biggest TNCs, though they operate worldwide, are still treated as if they belong to a particular "home country" and also happen to operate in other "host countries". The time has come to internationalize them formally—at least the biggest among them—and to put their obligations towards shareholders, employees, and other stakeholders on a fully international basis.

The one-world economy of the 21st century should, in fact, be equipped with company law at all its various levels—world, as well as continental (cf. the European company) and national—and perhaps even local, for small enterprizes which operate in one locality only. At the world level, a UN Code of Conduct for TNCs is now being negotiated. In due course, this Code should assume the status of international law, enforceable by an international administering authority through an international court. The appropriate administering authority might be a new International Trade Organization (see above), formed out of GATT and UNCTAD and the UN Commission on TNCs. Among the matters to be determined will be which companies should continue to be based simply on the national company laws of their home and host countries, which on international company law, and what the difference will be.

Notes and References

1. Keith V. Roberts, *A Design For A Market Economy*, Chapter 1, pp. 10–13. (Enquiries to: Mr. A.R.V. Roberts, Barn Cottage, Michelmersh, Romsey, Hants. SO51 0NR—tel. 0794 68387).

2. A series of New Economics Foundation seminars on Trade and Self-reliance organized by Pat Saunders of Quaker Peace and Service between January and May 1989 stimulated me to clarify my ideas on these and other issues discussed in this chapter.

3. Useful articles on international agricultural trade reform by Douglas Evans are in *New European Quarterly Review* (14/16 Carroun Road, London SW8 1ST), Winter 1987/88 and Winter 1988/89.

4. See Susan George, *A Fate Worse Than Debt*, Penguin 1988, for a full account.

5. Mohamed Idris, Martin Khor and their colleagues at Third World Network (87 Cantonment Road, 10250 Penang, Malaysia), and Edward Goldsmith and his colleagues, in the pages of *The Ecologist*, are among those who have been drawing the attention of concerned people to the damage done in many countries by the World Bank's policies.

6. For these and other facts see *Transnational Corporations in World Development: Trends and Prospects*, U.N. Centre on Transnational Corporations, U.N., New York, 1988.

8

Organizations

We have now looked at the implications of an enabling and conserving one-world economy for people and households, for local and national economies, and for the international economy. Enterprises and organizations of many kinds play a crucial role at all these levels.

Most people probably think of the business company as the typical economic organization, but governmental and third-sector organizations are just as significant. Our economic lives are largely shaped by the way all these organizations operate, the rules which govern them, the ways they take decisions, the flows of money to them and from them, the relationships between the people in them, and the relationships between them and the rest of society. So the question is how economic organizations—and the corporate economy as a whole—are to become enabling and conserving. That is what this chapter is about.

There are two key points to keep in mind. First, these organizations are for people. They are how people come together to achieve shared economic purposes. Second, the present structures and workings of these organizations are—no less than the present workings of the household, local, national and international economies—based on conditions and assumptions that are now historically out of date. If the underlying purpose of these organizations and the corporate economy as a whole is to enable and conserve—to create wealth and wellbeing for people and the Earth—rather than, say, to maximize monetary incomes and profits, big changes will be needed.

The Boredom Barrier Again

We noted in Chapter 1 that many people find economic discussion dismal and boring. Unfortunately, they find talk about economic organizations doubly so. Understandably. Organization talk is usually even more alienating for non-organization people than horse talk for the non-horsey or sailor talk for non-sailors. But we simply have to find ways of breaking through the boredom/mystification barrier. The structures of the corporate economy—the circuitry of the economic system—have to be redesigned to serve the real interests of people and the Earth.

Today's economic order and today's economic thinking tacitly assume, not that organizations are for people, but that people are for organizations, as employees, customers, taxpayers, investors, clients and so on. The great majority of economists, business people, politicians, public officials, academics and journalists look at economic questions from an organizational point of view. Most of them are employed by large organizations. They see the world, and their own place and future prospects in it, through organizational spectacles. They have a vested interest in today's organizations. So, in the first instance, change will have to be initiated from outside.

We should start by understanding that, by and large, the corporate economy today is dependency-creating, not enabling. It fosters personal and collective irresponsibility for removing poverty and social deprivation, for safeguarding local interests, and for conserving natural resources and the environment. One of the two opposing trends now taking place is making these faults worse. This is the trend towards bigger and more impersonal organizations, many of which give top priority to the maximization of financial success in an increasingly competitive international marketplace. The contrary trend towards smaller, more personally orientated organizations, which—though necessarily subject to the constraint of financial viability—are more closely concerned with meeting the real-life needs of real people in real places, is the one we have to encourage.

A three-pronged approach will be needed.

First, people responsible for the functioning of large organizations must be required to concern themselves with the benefits and costs—and the rights and obligations—of all the various different groups of people affected. Instead of aiming to maximize profit or benefit from the single notional point of view of a company or a nation, they must be required to optimize from the many different real-life points of view of all the various groups of people affected. The many large organizations that will continue to exist must be made much more responsive to the needs of all the people with whom they deal. They must become fully accountable for the effects they have on people and the natural environment.

Second, whenever possible, large organizations should be encouraged to split up into smaller autonomous organizations where people can feel they belong, work closely with their fellows, and share a sense of responsibility for their organization's dealings with the outside world.

Third, it must be made easier than it is today for people to set up their own organizations. People who want to come together in joint activities of their own choice should no longer have to depend on the expensive know-how of legal and financial specialists to make the necessary arrangements. That this is now the case is partly due to the muddled complexities of business law and finance, and partly to the tendency of legal and financial professionals to mystify such matters. But it also reflects most people's lack of education or training in economic self-reliance, and their resulting lack of capacity to self-organize. This is a natural feature of a dependency culture that conditions people to depend on employers to organize their work. It is one of the obstacles to be removed in the transition to an enabling economy.

Make-Up of the Corporate Economy

In order to design a well-functioning corporate economy for the 21st century, we need to understand the characteristics and functions of various different types of enterprises and organizations. To enable us to do this, we need to get organization experts to develop a comprehensive classification of organizations. That will put us in a position to discuss what mixture of different types of organization an enabling and conserving economy should contain.[1]

For example, types of organization include:

* multinational companies and banks;
* inter-governmental organizations like the World Bank;
* national companies;
* national government organizations and agencies;
* medium-sized and small commercial companies;
* local government organizations;
* charities and other non-commercial and non-governmental organizations like churches, trades unions, and all kinds of voluntary organizations and pressure groups;
* co-operatives, community businesses, credit unions, and other par- ticipatory organizations of that kind.

The question we must never lose sight of is, What are all these organizations for? The main characteristics of any organization are closely related to the answer. These include:

* its ownership and control;
* the nature and scale of its financial incomings and outgoings;
* its area of operations—local, national, international;
* its size;
* the nature of its activity—mining, banking, etc.

Before we take a closer look at these, we must dispose of an important red herring. It distorts our understanding of the corporate economy today. It is the false assumption that organizations fall into two distinct categories, economic and social, productive and non-productive, wealth-creating and wealth-consuming, and that these correspond to what are known as the private sector and public sector.

These simple distinctions are grossly over-simplified and misleading. It has become increasingly apparent in recent years that all organizations have a mixture of economic and social functions. Greater social awareness and a wish to contribute to social improvement have begun to take hold in parts of the commercial (or private) sector. Competitive market forces have begun to play a greater role in the public (or governmental) sector. And third-sector organizations, with mixed economic and social goals, have begun to play a more prominent part in the economy as a whole. The corporate economy can now be seen to consist of a variety of different types of organizations each with its own defining characteristics. And it is becoming evident that, if groupings are to be made, three—not two—clearly stand out: a governmental sector, corresponding to the existing public sector; a commercial sector, corresponding to the existing private sector; and a third, socio-economic, sector whose existence is now largely ignored by conventional economic thinkers and policy-makers.[2]

What Are These Organizations For?

The present situation is that, in practice as well as in theory, some business companies exist solely to make financial profits for shareholders. Their non-financial objectives are minimal. Other companies do, of course, have non-financial objectives—making motor cars, providing leisure facilities, or whatever. But company legislation in force in Britain today requires that, legally speaking, such non-financial objectives must be subordinate to the primary objective of maximizing the financial return to shareholders. As things now are, therefore, all normal business activity has to be orientated towards making money.

This raises many important and difficult questions for the future. How should company law be changed? Is the financial concept of profit outdated, as I argued fifteen years ago and as I still believe?[3] Should it be replaced by the more comprehensive idea that the cash flows generated by an organization should be distributed between all its stakeholders in accordance with its obligations to them? What would that mean for business motivation? How would capital accumulation then take place? What would profit and capital accumulation actually mean in an enabling and conserving economy? Can profits be made at all without imposing loss on someone else or on the Earth's resources? If an enabling and conserving economy was based on inflation-free and interest-free money (see Chapter 12) what difference would that make to our notions of profit? What would happen to stock exchange activity in a non-profit economy? Without the threat of profit-directed takeovers, what effective spur would there be to business efficiency?

All these questions will need to be worked through. A start should be made urgently in the early 1990s. Meanwhile, organizations which exist not primarily to make money but whose explicit primary objective is to provide a service of some kind or to achieve something in the real world, must—strictly speaking—take a form other than a shareholder company. They can be public-sector organizations, such as:

* a government department, which exists to serve the public;
* a nationalized industry, which exists to serve the public, but not mainly at public expense;
* a local government agency, which exists to serve the local public;
* a municipal enterprise, which exists to serve the local public, but not mainly at public expense.

Or they can be third-sector organizations, such as:

* a charity, which exists to perform specified charitable functions;
* a non-profit company, which exists to perform specified non-charitable functions;
* a consumer co-operative, which exists to provide goods and services to its customers;
* a worker co-operative, which exists to provide a livelihood for its workers;
* or a community business, which exists to meet needs of the local community.

We need to step up public discussion and promote wider public understanding in the 1990s about what these types of organisation, as well as business companies, are for. How should their objectives be defined, to ensure that they are enabling and conserving? How, in particular can third-sector organizations be encouraged, since these—such as co-operatives, community businesses, and voluntary organizations with mixed economic and social and environmental objectives—should by their nature be enabling and conserving? Phased programmes with target dates through the 1990s need to be drawn up for expanding the scale of their activity.

Ownership, Control and Finance

The ownership and control of organizations is closely linked with their economic and social objectives. Every organization has a range of different stakeholders—shareholders, workers, customers and so on. One type of organization tends to be controlled on behalf of its shareholders, another on behalf of its workers, another on behalf of its customers, another on behalf of the national state, another on behalf of the local state, another on behalf of the local community in which it operates, and another "mutually" on behalf of its customers and suppliers jointly. As it becomes increasingly necessary in many organizations, regardless which of the stakeholders has the controlling role, to recognize the rights of the others, the old argument between capitalism and socialism—should capital control labour or should labour control capital?—is clearly much too simple.

First, then, we need to develop more pluralistic and democractic structures of ownership and control, embodying the rights and obligations of all the various stakeholders in an organization.

Second, a piecemeal collection of special laws and regulations, difficult for anyone but specialists to understand, now governs all the various component organizations of the corporate economy, with their various mixes of financial and non-financial objectives and their various forms of ownership and control. This makes a happy hunting ground for corporate lawyers and accountants. In the 1990s we need to lay the foundations for a new, simpler, more comprehensive—and much more comprehensible—regulatory structure, systematically matched to the different economic and social objectives of different types of organization, their size, the nature of their business, and so on, and clearly defining the rights and obligations of the various categories of people who have dealings with them.

This will involve a redefinition of the financial structures of economic organizations. The financial structure of every organization reflects its ownership and control and its economic and social objectives. It affects an organization's responsiveness to the interests of its various stakeholders.

It must also be made easier for people setting up new organizations, especially in the third sector, to identify suitable sources of finance. Handbooks need to be written up for particular types of organization, showing how potential sources of finance can be matched to their potential needs, and giving guidance about how to raise "packages" of funding from varieties of different sources. New sources of finance for third-sector organizations are needed, and new channels through which people can invest in organizations of this type.

Various forms of popular capitalism must be encouraged, including wider share ownership and employee ownership.[4] So must various forms of decentralized socialism, including co-operatives and community-controlled companies.[5]

Scale, Size and Type of Business

Companies and other organizations may operate locally (i.e. in one locality), nationally (i.e. in a number of localities within one country), or multi-nationally (i.e. in a number of countries). When decisions about an organization's operations within a locality or nation are taken at a headquarters located elsewhere, the interests of people within the locality or nation take second place. The regulatory responsibilities of local, national and international government organizations in relation to local, national and multinational enterprises need to be rationalized. Work is needed to establish other ways in which local and national citizens and authorities can protect themselves from damaging decisions by companies and other economic organizations headquartered elsewhere.

The size of an organization can be measured in a number of different ways, including the number of people it employs, its capitalization value, its financial turnover, its annual profit, the number of its customers or clients, and the number of its shareholders or investors.

Criteria of size need to be worked out to which the legal and financial structure of organizations can be matched. The greater the impact of an organization on the outside world, the greater the need for it to operate openly in accordance with clearly understood rules governing the rights and obligations of all concerned. Too many disasters and financial scandals in recent years—Bhopal, Seveso, the Zeebrugge ferry disaster, the Kings Cross underground fire, the Guinness affair, the Exxon Alaska oil-spill, and so on—have demonstrated the irresponsibility and lack of accountability of top managements in large organizations.

In this context the effect of size on the performance—social and environmental, as well as financial—of companies and other economic organizations also needs to be documented. Conventional economics has been biased in favour of economies of scale. The 21st-century economy must pay more attention to the diseconomies and social costs of large scale and the economies and social benefits of small scale.

Of course, the nature of an organization's activity strongly influences its size and other characteristics. A different type of organization is necessary, for example, to run an international airline from the type needed to provide help with the care of sick people in their own homes. As an aspect of the proposed classification of organizations, research is needed on what types of organization will be best suited to what types of activity in an enabling and conserving economy.

Still on the question of size, the problem of monopolies will have to be tackled. It is pointless simply to transfer a monopoly from the public sector to the commercial sector, as has recently been done in Britain with the gas supply and the telephone service. These, and the supply of water and electricity, are bound to be monopolies so long as they continue to be based on technologies that require a system of pipes or wires which it would be wasteful, uneconomic and environmentally unacceptable for competitors to duplicate. Where monopolies are genuinely unavoidable, for physical or technical reasons, special arrangements for openness and public accountability must be rigorously enforced. But in the 21st-century economy the emphasis must be on breaking up monopolies whenever possible, and on developing decentralizing energy, communication, sewage and other technologies that will make this possible. This must be part of a comprehensive technological research and development effort to reduce the scale on which many production activities will be technically and economically viable.

Decision-Making and Motivation

How an organization reaches decisions and who is represented at what stages of the decision-making process, reflects the rights and obligations of the various stakeholders in the organization, the size and nature of the business, and so on. This is another aspect of the corporate economy which now needs to be opened up to public discussion. What decision-making structures and procedures are right for organizations of different types and sizes to ensure that they are enabling and conserving?

Decisions in most large organizations today are taken without giving full weight to social and environmental factors. For example, in deciding to build and equip a new factory, a company is guided primarily by production and marketing considerations. It is not aiming to achieve social or environmental benefits. Any social or environmental problems created by its decision will be dealt with only after the decision has been made. Hitherto, the techniques of social impact analysis, environmental impact analysis and technology assessment have been essentially defensive and remedial after the event.

Some years ago Eric Trist and his colleagues at the Tavistock Institute proposed a sociotechnical approach to the design of new work systems.[6] This would aim right from the start at a joint optimization of technical and social aspects—the social aspects, in this case, being limited to the quality of working life of the workers. But even that limited approach to the incorporation of social factors in company decision-making has never been widely adopted. It has not reflected actual corporate goals. In an enabling and conserving economy, social and environmental considerations will have to be brought into the early stages of corporate decision-making. Since this is only likely to be possible if social and environmental goals are among the primary goals of the organization, it raises many of the questions about corporate objectives, ownership, control and finance that we have touched on already.

How decisions are made is an aspect of the corporate context which vitally affects people's sense of commitment and responsibility for what they do. The corporate economy of the twenty-first century will have to provide more positive conditions for personal and organizational motivation than conventional capitalism and conventional socialism have provided.

The larger an organization, the greater the risk that careerist values, internal organizational demands, and alienation will divert the motivation of the people in it from the needs of the outside world. There are greater pressures on the ambitious, in their climb up the ladder, to harness their efforts to self-perpetuating and self-aggrandising organizational goals. There are greater pressures on the less ambitious conformists to play the system, since that is the surest way for them too to get their rewards. And there are greater pressures on those who feel the organization is exploiting them or failing to value them sufficiently, not to give of their best.

Even on their own terms, large organizations find it difficult to motivate people. Writing of high-risk industries like nuclear power, Charles Perrow says: "Organizational theorists have long since given up hope of finding perfect or even exceedingly well-run organizations, even where there is no catastrophic potential. It is an enduring limitation—if it is a limitation—of our human condition. It means that humans do not exist to give their all to organizations run by someone else . . . This is why it is not a problem of 'capitalism'; socialist countries . . . cannot escape the dilemmas of co-operative organized effort on any substantial scale and with any substantial complexity and uncertainty. At some point the cost of extracting obedience exceeds the benefits of organized activity."[7]

That these are strong arguments in favour of small organizations, can be attested by all who have worked in large ones. However, some large organizations will continue to exist, and the question of how they and the people in them can be motivated to be enabling and conserving is one that must be tackled. The issues include the following.

* Competition and co-operation: when and with whom and how should people be encouraged to compete, and when and with whom and how should they be encouraged to co-operate?
* Enterprise and accountability: how should people be encouraged to be enterprising, and at the same time be made accountable for what they do?

* Reward for performance: how can the rewards achieved by an organization and the people in it be made to match their performance? (The opposite often takes place, as when banks profit from their own dilatoriness in clearing cheques.)
* Risk-taking and reward: what risk-taking should be encouraged and what discouraged?

On the last point, today's economic order has encouraged corporate decision-makers to impose risks on other people, like the risks imposed on customers and third parties by the producers of tobacco and nuclear power. Just as limited liability has allowed shareholders to limit their financial risk with no corresponding limit to their prospect of financial gain, so corporate decision-makers in the pursuit of corporate and career success have been able to limit their personal liability for the risks they have taken with other people's wellbeing.

How, then, are we to insist on the liability of corporate decision-makers who take unjustified risks with other people's wellbeing? And how, conversely, can we adapt the 19th-century principle of limited liability in order to provide a measure of security to enterprising people whose initiatives are directed, not at creating profits for themselves and their shareholders, but at creating wealth and wellbeing for people and the Earth?

Business, Management and Organization Studies

Finally, business, management and organization have become important subjects for study, education and training in the past half-century. The emphasis has been, and still is, predominantly on how to make private-sector corporations more profitable, but public-sector management is also studied and taught professionally. For the future, greater emphasis will be needed on ways in which the commercial sector and the government sector can become enabling and conserving, on defining the rights and obligations of all the parties concerned (with the help of moral and political philosophers and jurisprudents), and on management training and education for people in the third sector—not forgetting training for household management, as suggested in Chapter 4.

Existing business schools, management centres, and organization specialists must be encouraged to take up the questions covered in this chapter. But some new institutions, combining the functions of think-tanks and pressure groups, will also be needed to provide a competitive stimulus.[8]

Notes and References

1. I first became aware of this need in the nineteen-seventies, when I did a study on the legal and financial structure of the enterprise for the Anglo-German

Foundation for the Study of Industrial Society. The "whole economy" perspective suggested by David Ross—see Paul Ekins (ed.), *The Living Economy*, RKP 1986, pp. 155 ff—now needs to be developed systematically in an enabling and conserving context.

2. The role of the third sector in the 21st-century economy was discussed in my 1987 Aves Memorial Lecture on "The Changing Environment of Volunteering", published by the Volunteer Centre, 29 Lower King's Road, Berkhamsted, Herts HP4 2AB.

3. See *Profit or People? The New Social Role of Money*, Calder and Boyars, 1974.

4. See David Howell, *Blind Victory: A Study in Income, Wealth and Power*, Hamish Hamilton, 1986. I strongly recommend this powerful argument for "the miniaturisation of capitalism, the spread of ownership into mass hands" from one of Mrs Thatcher's ex-Cabinet colleagues.

5. Martin Stott, *Beyond Isolation: Constructing a Co-ops Sector in the U.K. Economy*, ICOM (7–8 The Corn Exchange, Leeds LS1 7BP), 1986, and Paul Derrick, "Towards a Consensus on Common Ownership", *Science and Public Policy*, April 1985, are two useful recent accounts of prospects for co-operatives. Charles Knevitt (ed.), "Community Enterprise"—a booklet with a foreword by the Prince of Wales—published by *The Times* and the Gulbenkian Foundation in 1986, is a useful introduction to community businesses. Strathclyde Community Busines and Community Business Scotland, Six Harmony Row, Govan, Glasgow are valuable sources of information on community businesses in the U.K.

6. Eric L. Trist. "The Sociotechnical Perspective", Chapter 2 of *Perspectives on Organization Design and Behaviour*, eds. Van de Ven and Joyce, Wiley 1981.

7. Charles Perrow, *Normal Accidents: Living with High-Risk Technologies*, Basic Books, New York, 1984, pp. 338–339. Diana Schumacher drew my attention to this study, when I was preparing a paper on "The Changing Environment for Safety and Risk at Work" for an international safety conference in Montreal in June 1988.

8. The Business Network (18 Well Walk, Hampstead, London NW3 1LD) is a valuable source of relevant information and ideas.

9

Money

Money is crucial. It links the component parts of the economy with one another. The way it does this, and how the money system functions, goes far to determine the character of the economy as a whole.

Chapters 4 to 8 have mentioned money as an aspect of the economic activities of individuals and households, local and national economies, the international economy, and organizations of all kinds. Those chapters suggested changes in how those component parts of the economy each use money and take decisions about it, as part of the transition to an enabling and conserving economy.

In this chapter and the three which follow we look at money from a wider perspective—as if we were cosmonauts looking down from space on the operations of the money system in the economy of planet Earth. Our concern here is wider than just the role which money plays in the affairs of the economy's individual component parts. It is with the changes needed in the way we think about money and in the way the money system works as a whole. This chapter discusses the need for a new understanding of the economic functions of money. The two following chapters discuss two particularly important features of the money system that help to determine its economic impacts—taxation and the distribution of incomes and capital. Then Chapter 12 asks whose money system it is anyway, and takes up the need for changes in regard to currencies, interest and debt.

Reform of the money system will be central to the transition to an enabling and conserving economy. Economic development in recent centuries has brought with it a continuing expansion of money-based transactions into areas of human activity in which relationships were previously based on gift and custom, reciprocity and mutual aid. Money now plays a central part in the economic life of the world and of the majority of people in it. It will continue to do so for as far ahead as we can see, even if we envisage—as we do—a larger role for informal economic activities in which money plays no part.

Money as Master

The money system now operates in ways directly contrary to the needs of an enabling and conserving economy.

Take conserving first. Today's money system positively encourages the rapid consumption of resources. In any particular case—say a particular quantity of oil—the money gained from extracting or using it today will tend to be worth more than the money to be expected from leaving it unused for the time being. If the sum acquired today from selling or otherwise using the oil can be banked at 10 per cent interest per annum, the money will double its value—with compound interest—in less than nine years' time. So if 10 per cent is the going interest rate now and there is any risk that the value of the unused oil will not double in nine years' time, it is a better financial bet to realise its value now than to conserve it, to have the money now rather than later.

This explains the practice of discounting the present worth of future money. It means that—from a conventional economic point of view—revenues and costs arising in the rather longer-term future are not worth considering at all. So, as a matter of normally accepted practice today, conventional business planning and conventional economic analysis ignore anything that may happen further into the future than twenty or thirty years—including any effects of destroying natural resources and polluting the environment. This very serious problem is directly linked to the fact that if you have money and save it you get paid interest, but if you have natural resources and save them you don't. The practice of charging and paying interest is now generally accepted as a natural fact of monetary life. It must be questioned—see Chapter 12.

So far as enabling is concerned, the money system—as it now operates—restricts the economic capacity and freedom of many people and places and nations by making them dependent on getting money incomes from sources over which they have no control. By the way they regulate money and finance, government agencies and monetary authorities often make it more difficult for people to work in the informal economy—see Chapter 4. Historically, by imposing monetary taxes on subsistence farmers, rulers compelled them to work as paid labourers for larger landowners to get the necessary tax money, instead of working unpaid for themselves to improve their own and their families' living. Just so today, governments like the British government insist that, in order to be eligible for benefits, unemployed people must be ready and available to accept paid work from employers, regardless of any more socially or environmentally useful unpaid work they otherwise might do. At the other end of the scale, international monetary authorities similarly impose conditions on nations, restricting their freedom to decide their own economic policies and pushing them deeper into economic dependency. The IMF's insistence that indebted

Third World countries should concentrate on exporting commodities fetching low world prices to richer nations, rather than on producing goods for their own people, is a current example.

The role of debt in creating and reinforcing economic dependency needs no elaboration. A debtor has to find money not only to repay the principal owed but also the interest payable on it. Unless the interest is regularly paid, the amount of the debt increases and dependency deepens. Debt and interest are key factors in dependency creation, as in ecological wastefulness.

But, quite apart from debt, it is important to get it widely recognized that the growing role of money in the lives of individual people and in the workings of human society as a whole over the last 200 years has brought increased economic dependence. As I said in Chapter 1, modern development began when enclosures of the common land deprived the "common people" in countries like Britain of the means to provide a subsistence livelihood for themselves and their families, and made them dependent on paid labour. The same process continues today in those regions of the world—mainly equatorial, arctic and mountainous—where millions of hitherto non-industrialized and tribal peoples are having their traditional environments and ways of life destroyed by logging, oil pipelines, big dams and other forms of development, and are being made dependent on work as wage-labourers or on welfare handouts from the state.

It is not just the unfortunate and the oppressed who have become more dependent on money in this way. We are all, almost without exception, more dependent on money than our ancestors were. Whereas in pre-industrial times most people, living in rural village communities, provided most of the necessities of life for themselves and one another directly through their own work, most people in modern society are almost wholly dependent on money for the goods and services they need—either to purchase them themselves or to be provided with them by public services paid for with public money.

So much so that, as I have pointed out elsewhere,[1] money now plays the central role in late industrial society that religion played in the late Middle Ages. Then the local church was the most prominent building in most villages; today the prime sites in every high street are occupied by branches of banks, building societies, and other financial concerns. The centres of medieval cities were dominated by cathedrals; today's city centres are dominated by the tower blocks of international banks. Today's army of accountants, bankers, tax-people, insurance brokers, stock jobbers, foreign exchange dealers and countless other specialists in money, is the modern counterpart of the medieval army of priests, friars, monks, nuns, abbots and abbesses, pardoners, summoners and other specialists in religious procedures and practices. The theologians of the late Middle Ages have their counterpart in the economists of the late industrial age. Then they argued about how to measure the space occupied by angels; now they argue about how to measure unemployment or the money supply. Financial complexity holds us in thrall today, as religious complexity held our ancestors then. Just look at the financial pages of the daily newspapers—especially on Saturdays.

As the role of money has become greater in the lives of people and society, the institutions set up to handle money have become bigger and more remote. In step with increasing centralization in industry and government, financial institutions have become more centralized. Small local banks have been taken over by bigger banks and turned into local branches of national banking networks. Only in very exceptional cases are local financial institutions found today with the function of channelling local money into investment in local enterprises and projects. So it is not just individual people who have become more dependent on money coming in and going out again. The same is true of places, like cities and rural districts. And also of nations. There has never before been a Third World debt crisis like the one there is now.

Impersonal and Amoral

With this growing dependence on money has come a growing impersonality and lack of positive morality in the use of money. As we noted in Chapters 4 and 5, the investment of money has become less personal and less local, as has the spending of money in supermarkets instead of local corner shops, and the earning of money from faceless employing organizations instead from personal employers. As increasing numbers of people have acquired savings to invest—in pensions for their retirement and in mortgages for their houses, as well as in other forms of saving—they have not been expected to take a personal interest in how those savings are used. Just as employees have become content to hand over responsibility to employing organizations to direct the purposes of their work, so savers have been content to hand over responsibility to a bank, or a pension fund, or a building society, or some other financial institution, to decide what use is to be made of their money.

With this has gone a growing tendency to try to make money out of money rather than out of useful activity. This has resulted in the huge growth of stock markets, money markets, bond markets, currency markets and other financial markets throughout the world, and in the ever-growing demand for capital assets like land and property, not mainly to make good use of them but in the hope of selling them later at a capital gain. And this in turn has been one of the contributing factors to the massive expansion of borrowing and debt—personal, corporate, national and international—that has taken place in the last thirty or forty years.

The fact that money has become more abstract and less material, as discussed below, has reinforced the growing impersonality of our use of money and our dependence on it. We have now become very largely dependent on the banking and financial institutions' computerized communications networks, through which money transactions are carried out simply by crediting and debiting the accounts of the parties to the transaction. The whole process is far removed from the old way of making payments by the hand-to-hand, person-to-person transfer of coin and paper. We now have a world money system in which the money markets and stock markets of Tokyo, London and New York are linked in a continually active web of financial transactions twenty-four hours a day. Many of these transactions are activated automatically, by computers programmed to buy and sell currencies and bonds, stocks and shares, when price levels reach a certain point. The people operating the system and carrying out the transactions know nothing and care nothing about the lives of the people ultimately affected by these financial transactions. Not for nothing did Martin Buber ask, "Can the servant of Mammon say Thou to his money?".[2]

A Bird's-Eye View

It is natural enough, the way the monetary and financial system has evolved, that no-one should have been very interested in how to design it and manage it efficiently and fairly in the interests of all its users. The immediately important thing for everyone is to make sure that we have enough money coming in to match what we need to spend out. How can we get more and, if necessary, spend less? If we don't get this right, we are in trouble. The same is true for companies and other organizations. And, disappointing though it may be, it applies to governments too. Throughout history, rulers and governments have been much more interested in using the money system to their own advantage than in trying to make it work efficiently and fairly for all concerned.

This affects the orientation of almost all who are especially knowledgeable about money and finance, or professionally expert in some aspect of it. If they do not use their knowledge and expertise to make more money for themselves, they will use it to advise other people or companies or governments how to do so. And the vast majority of academic and journalistic commentators on monetary and financial matters are interested in them from that standpoint. I now understand this. But when in the late nineteen-sixties I went to run the Inter-Bank Research Organization for the big banks in the City of London, I was surprised that so very few of the financial experts, economic commentators and monetary academics I came across, understood or were interested in how the whole system works. How the monetary and financial system as a whole helps to shape economic life and how it actually does so today, what its functions should be, and how its further evolution could lead to its carrying out those functions more effectively—these were questions that featured on nobody's agenda.[3]

Unfortunately, things have not changed much for the better in this respect in the last twenty years.

To bring these questions on to the agenda now, we must take—as I have said—the cosmonauts' bird's-eye view. When we do this, we shall see the money system from a fresh perspective. Sometimes it will look to us like an information system, and we shall interpret the way it works as if that is what it is. This will be in tune with up-to-date scientific thinking, which now successfully models many aspects of the natural and man-made world in terms of informatics and information systems. Sometimes it will look to us more like a network of flows—of cash flows, that is—linking all the people and organizations taking part in economic life, reflecting and helping to shape their relationships with one another. Again, we shall be in tune with up-to-date scientific thinking which now tends to see the world in ecological or systems terms, as consisting primarily of interactions and relationships rather than of free-standing entities. The fact that it sometimes seems useful to see the money system as an information system and sometimes as a network of flows, should not disturb us. At certain stages of understanding this kind of double vision is helpful, as in physics earlier this century when it was sometimes helpful to interpret light as particles and sometimes as waves.

Money as Information

The evolution of money has, as we have just noted, been from concrete to abstract: from valuables like cattle and tobacco; to metal bars and coins; to paper notes and cheques; and now to numbers electronically stored in computer files and electronically transmitted between them. As this last stage has arrived—with the transformation of monetary and financial assets into entries in computerized accounts, and of monetary and financial transactions into electronic messages that debit and credit the accounts of payer and payee—our understanding of the nature of money and its role in economic life is reaching a watershed.

So long as people were required to transfer money to one another in the form of actual things, such as metal and paper, this gave colour to the idea that money was itself a kind of thing—a commodity like other commodities. Concepts like the money supply and the velocity of circulation of money then seemed to make sense, in spite of the difficulties of measuring them satisfactorily. So did the concept of money as something that had to be issued and put into circulation. So did the idea of tying the value of a currency to the value of a commodity like gold, or to the value of a "basket" of commodities in more general use, like grain or timber.

But now it is becoming clear that the monetary and financial system is basically an information system. Money and finance provide an accounting system, or scoring system, which regulates people's economic relations with one another. It indicates the claims for goods and services which people are entitled to make on one another, it enables them to trade those claims in exchange for goods and services, and it enables them (e.g. through investment and insurance) to exchange their present claims (such as money in a bank account) for other financial claims (such as an equity shareholding in a commercial company, or a life policy or accident policy with an insurance company).

This last point about the exchange of financial claims is important. The financial system consists predominantly of the wide variety of traders and brokers who have come into existence over the years to create a market—or otherwise provide facilities—for exchanging financial claims of this kind. They include all kinds of financial institutions—banks, building societies, insurance companies, stockbrokers, unit trusts, foreign exchange dealers, and many, many others. In principle, the financial system can offer an almost infinite variety of possible deals for lending and borrowing, investing and insuring, exchanging one currency for others, and so on—all of which involve paying (or receiving) a certain amount of a certain kind of money at a certain time, in return for the right to receive (or the obligation to pay) a certain amount of a certain kind at a certain time under certain conditions. New sorts of deals, defined by particular sets of options and conditions that have not been available before, are continually being thought up and introduced by financial innovators.

This sounds rather good. But there are a couple of flaws. Both are directly connected with the fact that making money out of money has become so profitable.

First, the people and organizations who run the financial system are in it primarily to make money out of it for themselves—in other words, to distort its functioning in their own interests and those of their customers and associates. They don't technically cook the books—not most of them, that is. But collectively they cook the whole system. Yuppies and others who go into banking and the City do so to get higher salaries and make more money for themselves than they could elsewhere, not to dedicate themselves to managing and operating an efficient and fair monetary and financial system to facilitate the workings of the economy in the interest of all. In other words, the financial system that exists today is systemically corrupt.

Second, again because it is so profitable, the volume of activity and the number of people employed in the financial system has grown to cancerous proportions. It is estimated, for example, that only about 5 per cent of the foreign exchange transactions that now take place are related to international trading transactions in non-financial goods and services. Ninety-five per cent are to do simply with making money out of money. This is rather as if the game of cricket were to develop to the point where the one or two people, who keep score of the activities of the twenty-two out on the field, were joined in the scorers' box by an ever-increasing number of the players; as if these, by using the runs scored by their remaining team-mates as stakes in gambling and betting games of various kinds, were then able to achieve a twentyfold increase in their side's score; and as if—for obvious reasons—the gamblers and betsmen then became more sought after, better paid and more highly regarded than the bowlers and batsmen. The nature of the game would change. And for the worse.

A Network of Flows

The other way of seeing the monetary and financial system is as a worldwide network of cash flows connecting people and organizations of all kinds. The way this network functions reflects and determines the workings of the economy. The way it functions is determined partly by the behaviour of its nodes, that is all the millions of people and organizations in the world who transmit and receive money to and from one another, and partly by the characteristics of the network as a whole. So, to improve the way it functions, we need to improve it in both these respects.

In Chapter 4 I suggested that, as consumers and savers, and also as earners, we should use our purchasing, saving and earning power purposefully, to help to create the kind of world and the kind of future we want. To support and inform this purposeful use of our economic power, we need to visualize how our patterns of earning and spending link us into the wider activity patterns of society and the world. Each one of us receives inward payments from other people and organizations—as wages, salaries or fees for work, as pensions and social security benefits, as dividends and interest on our savings, as gifts and prizes, as the proceeds from sales of property and possessions or from realizing savings, and so on. And each one of us makes outward payments for such things as food, clothing, household expenses, transport, holidays and leisure, mortgages, insurance premiums, taxes, purchases of shares or units in unit trusts, and so on. Everyone from whom we receive money and everyone who receives it from us has a comparable set—a comparable pattern—of payments in and out. So does everyone from whom they receive money and everyone who receives it from them. And so on, extending to the great majority of human beings now alive. Each of us is a nodal point on this great network of money transactions, actual and potential, that holds human society together, both expressing and helping to shape its dominant patterns of behaviour and its impacts on the world.

The sets of inward and outward payments linking each node—that is each one of us, each economic entity—into that global network, both reflect and shape the part we each play in the economy and the impact we each have on it. By the way we each control and direct our own pattern of payments in and out, we each help to shape what happens in the world. All economic entities—people and households, cities and other localities, nations, and commercial, governmental and third-sector organizations of every kind—share this basic feature. Every one has flows of money coming in and money going out. The sources and destinations and sizes and frequencies of all these flows of money shape and reflect the wider economy. The pattern of the flows is shaped by choices made by each node on the network, by each node with which it transacts, and so on through the world economy as a whole.

Many of the points made in Chapters 4 to 8 were related to this concept of the economy—or, to be precise, the formal economy—as a worldwide network of money flows linking all people and organizations. One, as I have just said, is to do with the purposeful workers, consumers and savers of Chapter 4. Then in Chapters 5, 6 and 7 I suggested changes in patterns of public spending and taxation by local governments, national governments, and international government agencies. In Chapter 8 I suggested a need for more open and representative methods and procedures in businesses and other economic organizations for deciding and controlling their flows of money out and in.

The idea is taken up again in the three chapters that now follow, this time in the context of a number of specifically financial issues that are of central importance—taxation and public expenditure; the distribution of income and capital; currencies; interest, credit and debt; and the future development of financial institutions. Meanwhile, however, I want to stress again the need to focus public concern on the matters discussed in this chapter.

The Top Priority

The top priority for the 1990s is to foster widespread public interest in the way the money and financial system actually works, how it will need to work in an enabling and conserving economy, and what changes this will require. The following points need to be established in the public mind.

First, the proper function of money and finance is to enable all the billions of people who take part in economic activities all over the world to carry out economic transactions and to conduct economic relations with one another. The monetary and financial system does this by providing a system of linked accounts (and cash in the form of paper and metal tokens) through which people anywhere in the world can transfer financial claims between one another, either in exchange for real goods and services or in exchange for other different financial claims.

Second, the monetary and financial system has developed historically in such a way that it has never been properly designed to carry out this function efficiently and fairly. The primary concern of the goldsmiths and bankers and government servants who have built it up over the centuries, and of the bankers and other financial specialists who operate it today, has been to make money for themselves and their organizations, and their customers, shareholders and other associates. No wonder that its overall impact is now disabling and ecologically destructive. It encourages everyone to try to get more for themselves at the expense of other people and the natural environment.

Third, since money can be understood as information about the claims for goods and services that people and organizations are entitled to make on one another, the monetary and financial system needs to be designed and operated as an information system—a fair and efficient scoring system. Insights from the design, management and operation of information and communication systems should be brought to be bear upon the changes now needed in it.

Fourth, visualizing the patterns of payments transmitted by people and organizations to one another as a worldwide network, reflecting the patterns of real economic activity taking place all over the world and shaped by the spending and earning decisions of each person and organization, throws light on many of the changes that will need to be made in the transition to a new economic order.

Finally, ministers and politicians, officials of government monetary authorities, and directors and managers of financial institutions, all have public responsibilities for the way the monetary and financial system works. We must press them, and also academic economists and other financial specialists, to tell us what changes they think are needed. How do they think the monetary and financial system should be redesigned and further evolved to operate efficiently and fairly as a vital part of an enabling and conserving multi-level global economy? How do they think it should be managed, so that those who operate it do so in the general public interest instead of their own?

Notes and References

1. *Future Work*, pp. 126 ff.
2. Martin Buber, *I and Thou*, Scribner, New York, 1958, p. 106. As I said, in an unpublished paper on "Money: I, Thou And It", given at a conference for the Teilhard Centre on 3rd October 1987, this insight of Buber's is relevant to an

apparent paradox in the Teilhardian vision. The emergence of a worldwide money transmission network is clearly part of what Teilhard saw as the emerging noosphere or global mind. Yet it represents a process of depersonalization, not personalization as Teilhard assumed noogenesis would be.

3. My experience at that time strengthened my earlier impression that the monetary and financial system is in need of more radical restructuring than is generally envisaged, for example by politicians of the Left. See *Profit or People? The New Social Role Of Money*, Calder and Boyars, 1974. Also *Power, Money and Sex: Towards New Social Balance*, Marion Boyars, 1976.

10

Taxes

Governments—local, national, international—have even more scope than other economic agents to shape economic development for better or for worse by the ways they direct the flows of payments to and from themselves.

The most important payments received by governments are taxes. Governments determine the basis for these payments. This chapter suggests how the principles of enabling and conserving will apply to a multi-level—local, national and international—taxation system, and what now needs to be done about it. (Public borrowing provides another important inflow of funds to governments. We will mention it again shortly, and again in Chapter 12.)

Outward flows of payments from governments are public spending. Other chapters have suggested the need for changes there. Chapter 4 suggested that—in place of existing social benefits—a universal basic income, paid by government to every citizen as of right, would eliminate many of the disabling and dependency-creating effects of conventional economic and social policies. Chapter 11 takes that discussion further. Chapters 5 and 6 suggested a systematic shift of emphasis at both local and national government levels to spending programmes that enable and conserve. Chapter 13 will give some specific examples. Chapter 7 mentioned the need to systematize public spending programmes at the global level, by the United Nations and associated organizations.

This chapter will not be dealing with public expenditure or public borrowing. However, in dealing with taxation, we do need to keep them in mind. The equation "public spending = taxation + public borrowing" means that each of the three helps to determine the other two. It is in combination with the other two that each produces the economic impact it does. There must be a coherent, sensibly designed system for handling them together, in combination, at each level of government. It should be based on procedures that enable people and their elected representatives to understand and discuss the combined economic effect of their governments' public spending, taxation and borrowing policies.

This was the point on which I wrote in 1971, with reference to the British Treasury, revenue departments and Bank of England: "Eventually, before we are all dead, God willing, they will be able to combine these separate systems for planning, managing and reviewing expenditure, taxation and borrowing into a unified system for controlling them in combination. Only then shall we be able to talk realistically about steering the economy in the desired direction."[1] Alas! little progress has yet been made. At the time of writing, Mrs Thatcher's government is still presenting its public spending proposals to Parliament for debate in the autumn, and its revenue proposals at Budget time in the spring. No-one running a corner shop would handle their cash flow projections in such an eccentric way as that.

There is one further point to be made here about public expenditure. In the long term, as the emphasis in government policies shifts away from direct intervention and provision of services to ways of enabling people to be more self-reliant and conserving, aggregate levels of public expenditure over the years are likely to fall—at least in real terms. Required levels of taxation (and public borrowing) will come down accordingly. This is one aspect of the crucially significant negative multiplier effect which, as explained in Chapter 12, will be a feature of the transition to an enabling and conserving economy.

Objectives of the Tax System

The tax system for an enabling and conserving one-world economy will differ in important ways from today's. In addition to raising the revenue needed to support the expenditure of government authorities, it should be designed:

* to encourage people to develop their productive capacities, to use them for the common good, and to become more self-reliant in the provision of goods and services for themselves and one another;
* to encourage organizations to enable people to develop their productive capacities in that way;
* to encourage local and, especially in the Third World, national economies to become more self-reliant too;
* to encourage efficient use, fair distribution and conservation of scarce resources, and discourage waste, pollution and other socially and environmentally harmful behaviour;
* to be progressive and redistributive, in the sense of taking more from rich individuals, localities and nations than from poor, and redistributing income and wealth from rich to poor—but without reducing the

incentives for anyone, however rich or poor, to make an effective contribution to meeting their own and other people's needs.

It must also be designed:

* to be simple enough for people to understand without needing tax experts to tell them how it works, and without therefore spawning a great army of tax accounting specialists—who might otherwise use their lives in materially and socially more useful, and spiritually more rewarding, ways;
* to be non-discriminatory between different categories of citizen, e.g. between men and women, and—in the international economy— between different nations.

A Fundamental Shift

The over-riding priority is to secure widespread understanding and acceptance of the idea that the burden of taxation must be shifted away from what people contribute to the rest of society and on to what they take from it—that is to say, shifted away from useful work which adds value, and on to occupation of land, use of energy and resources, and activities that risk imposing waste, pollution, ill health, and other environmental and social costs on the rest of society. The task is to formulate clearly the long-term changes in the present taxation system that this will imply, to study their feasibility in practical terms, and to work out how they should be phased in over a period of years.

We should not try to conceal the fundamental nature of what we are proposing. Among other things, it will be a shift away from taxing the shadow—the artificial mirror economy of money incomes, value added, profits, capital gains, capital transfers, and so on—to taxing the substance—the real economy in which, when some people occupy land, or use and waste natural resources, or pollute the environment, they do so to the exclusion and detriment of others. As a working hypothesis, we should envisage the eventual removal of all taxes on incomes and value added, savings and financial capital—resulting in no personal or company taxes as such, no VAT, and no capital taxes including capital gains or capital transfer taxes.

This means than no-one will be taxed on money as such—either the money that comes in as income or profit or the financial assets they already possess. This will help to eliminate the poverty trap for the poor and the disincentive for the not-so-poor of, as they see it, the state confiscating well-earned money that rightfully belongs to them. Taxes will much more nearly take the form of rents and charges reasonably paid in exchange either for the use of resources that would otherwise be available for other people, or for damage caused to other people. Taxation will thus come to be seen in a different way from how most people see it today.

This change will also help to eliminate the present tax bias which favours the business sector against household and other informal production—see Chapter 4. This bias arises from the fact that, with taxes on incomes and profits, the costs of materials and equipment used by the business sector in the production of goods and services for sale are met from untaxed money, i.e. they can be set off against taxed profits, whereas the corresponding costs of producing the same goods and services in the household or elsewhere for direct consumption have to be met out of taxed income.

The change will also mean, of course, that no-one—whether persons or companies or other organizations such as charities—would receive tax allowances or tax exemptions. Any valid purposes for which tax allowances and exemptions are at present used would have to be achieved in other ways. For example, personal tax allowances would be replaced by the basic income paid unconditionally to all citizens—see Chapter 11. By setting this, and the taxes on occupation of land and use of energy and resources, at high enough levels, the government of the day would be able to achieve a very powerful progressive and redistributive effect in real economic terms. There would be no need to complicate the tax system with additional taxes for that purpose. Any further redistributive measures could be taken by replacing regressive and dependency-reinforcing public spending programmes with enabling ones, including measures to spread the ownership of land and capital more widely.

A key task for the early 1990s will be to stimulate public discussion of the need to shift the burden of taxation as proposed here. This will require the working up of quite detailed practical proposals. The following are some of the questions on which feasibility studies are needed, to demonstrate the practicability and probable consequences of what is being proposed.

Occupation of Land

The proposal is for a tax on the site-value of all land, the site-value being the value of any plot or area of land in its unimproved state, i.e. excluding the value of any buildings on it or other man-made improvements that have been made to it. The tax will be paid annually by the owners of the land. It will be calculated as a percentage of the capital value of the site or of its annual rental value. This will, in effect, be a tax on every piece of land at the point just before it contributes to any economic activity. It will therefore enter into the cost of every activity involving that piece of land, including the cost of leaving it idle. Not only will it capture for the community a proportion of any communally created increase in land values. It will tend to encourage efficient land use, to reduce the value of land in relation to other forms of capital, to redistribute wealth as well as income from those who own valuable city-centre and agricultural land to those who don't, and make it easier for more people to own a piece of land.

This tax was first proposed by the 19th-century American economist Henry George, who argued—as we do not—that, if it were introduced, no other taxation would be needed at all. I am not going to set out here the very wide-ranging economic, social and environmental arguments in its favour. I have done so in *Future Work*, and other useful references are given in *The Living Economy*.[2] Site-value taxation was for many years included among Liberal Party policies and is currently supported by the Green Party in the UK.

Later in this chapter I suggest that this tax should be a combined local and national tax. But to get to it generally accepted that any form of tax on the site value of land is a practical proposition, we must be able to give properly researched answers to the following questions:

* What total revenue could be raised from an annual tax on the site-value of all the land in the locality or the nation, if the tax rate (i.e. the percentage of annual rental value payable annually as tax) were set at 25%, 50%, 75%, or 100%?
* What repercussions on economic activity might such a tax at such tax levels be expected to have?
* What would need to be done to make it administratively feasible to raise this tax?

Energy and Resources

Ernst von Weizsacker, the Director of the Institute for European Environmental Policy,[3] is among those who have proposed that the tax burden should be shifted from labour to energy and resources. Farel Bradbury is another.[4]

Bradbury's proposal is that energy should be taxed at source, that is at the point of its entry into the economy. The tax would be calculated, not as a percentage of the monetary value of the energy, but in relation to its calorific value.

Bradbury has worked out that Europe, including the U.K., could entirely replace value-added-tax (VAT) by an energy tax of this kind set at a rate of £1.15 per gigajoule of source energy. This energy tax would, of course, be passed on by energy producers to their customers, and by them to their customers, and so on right through every stage of economic activity to final consumers of goods and services. It would thus have a conserving effect on all economic activity. It would be progressive in the sense that people and organizations, including shareholders in companies, using greater quantities of more energy-intensive goods and services would be contributing more to taxation than people using, or benefiting from the use of, less. Assuming that it would be a national tax, it would be very much simpler to collect than VAT or, for that matter, than income tax.

As with the site-value tax on land, it is not difficult to understand in general principle that an energy tax on these lines would have a beneficial overall effect—as a substitute for, not an addition to, VAT and other taxes. But, again, the practical task now is to show how such a tax would actually work, and what its detailed effects would be likely to be. Feasibility studies are needed to give authoritative answers to questions such as the following.

* How would a tax on the first introduction of energy into the economy actually be collected? Which types of companies (and private persons, if any) would pay the tax to the tax authorities? What problems would have to be ironed out—e.g. to distinguish between renewable and non-renewable energy sources, or in relation to the fuel and non-fuel uses of substances such as wood, biomass and petroleum-based chemical feedstocks? What would have to be done to make this tax administratively feasible?
* What total revenue could this tax be expected to raise, at various different rates of tax? What other taxes could it, therefore, replace?
* What repercussions on economic activity and existing economic interests might such a tax, at various rates of tax, be expected to have?

The possible merits and feasibility of similar taxes at source on non-energy resources and materials—whether in the form of depletion taxes or saleable depletion quotas or licences, as Herman Daly has proposed[5]—also need to be worked through. Are these necessary in addition to the energy tax? Would they apply to all mining and quarrying of minerals, stone, sand and gravel? And what about forest, agricultural and fishery products? And water? How much revenue could such taxes be expected to raise? What would have to be done to make them administratively feasible?

Waste and Pollution

The scope for taxes on activities which cause, or risk causing, waste and pollution and harm to other people needs to be carefully worked through. These activities include the creation of waste and rubbish that has to be cleaned up, pollution of air, soil, and water, and the creation of noise, vibration and smell. They include much that comes under the headings of occupational and environmental health and safety. They might also be taken to include such things as the erosion of soil from one's own or other people's land, and the sale of health-damaging products like alcohol and tobacco.

The need is to make the waster and the polluter pay. There is no argument about this. It is necessary in order to discourage waste and pollution, to contribute to the cost of remedial measures, and to penalize activities that cause damage, ill-health and nuisance in the widest sense. In economists' language these are activities that externalize important costs, i.e. impose them on other people. The aim must be to internalize them, by bringing them home in one way or another to those who are responsible for them. The question is how best to do this, and what part taxes should play.

It is possible to imagine a proliferation of special taxes inflicting penalties of varying severity on a multitude of different wasting and polluting activities—heavier taxes on leaded than unleaded petrol, on coal than on cleaner energy sources, on noisier than quieter machinery and vehicles and aircraft, on packaged goods that cause litter than on unpackaged goods that don't, on fertilisers and pesticides that can poison food and water and air than on those that can't, and so on. It is also possible to imagine recoverable taxes on an almost unlimited range of manufactured products—cars, refrigerators, tables, cans, bottles, you name it—the tax being reclaimable if the last owner of a product, instead of throwing it away or dumping it, returns it to a state agency for recycling. Some people find this approach attractive. Certainly, it could provide meat and drink for a small army of environmental economists and bureaucrats.

Before a convincing case can be made for this kind of wide range of special taxes on pollution, it will be necessary for feasibility studies to answer the following questions.

* What pollution taxes are envisaged?
* How would these taxes actually work, and what would have to be done to make them administratively feasible?
* What revenue could they be expected to raise?

However, although an argument can no doubt be made for this detailed case-by-case tax strategy to fight waste and pollution, there may be less complex ways of achieving the desired result. For example, the generalized land and energy taxes outlined earlier will be much more pervasive than the effects of special pollution taxes, because land and energy taxes will bear upon the basic physical ingredients of all economic activities, not just the end results of some. The energy tax will automatically reduce the volume of waste and pollution—much of which represents wasted energy—and will encourage many manufacturers to save energy by producing and using recyclable goods and giving incentives to customers to return them after use. Moreover, it will often be simpler and more effective to reduce pollution by banning it and then fining and imprisoning those who break the law, than by taxing it. Indeed, it can be argued that to tax pollution as such would be, in a sense, to legitimize it; and that it is preferable to make it illegal and penalize it by fining or imprisonment. No amount of taxation should be allowed to justify pollution on the scale of the Union Carbide disaster at Bhopal or the Exxon oilspill in Alaska.

Local Taxation

Local government should enjoy a defined degree of autonomy in relation to national government, in taxation as in other matters. A local authority's spending should therefore be met from taxes which are either raised by the local authority itself or which come to it as of right, rather than as grants and handouts to be negotiated each year with the national government. At the same time the national government must carry out the important redistributive function of providing poorer local authority areas with some of the tax money raised from richer ones. How are these two requirements both to be met in a reformed system of local and national taxation?

In Britain the property rating system on which local government taxation has been based is currently being replaced, first by a community charge (or poll tax) payable to the local government authority by each individual local resident regardless of income and wealth, and second by a rate payable by businesses to the national government which will distribute the proceeds to local authorities. These arrangements are likely to prove unsatisfactory and perhaps unworkable in the course of the 1990s. But to return to a property rating system of the previous kind will also be unacceptable. There is an opportunity here to move forward, which we must be ready to take.

In preparation for it, the possibility to be examined is that a land tax (as outlined earlier in this chapter), perhaps in combination with a local personal tax developed out of the community charge, could provide the basis for local government taxation. (The personal tax would be used as a subsidiary tax, to top up the proceeds of the land tax. It would be levied by local authorities at whatever rate each decided annually, in accordance with electoral opinion in their locality.)

The tax on land will have to be nationally based, or at least there will have to be a national element in it, so that some of the tax raised from richer parts of a country—as, in Britain, the City of London—can be redistributed to poorer parts like the Highlands of Scotland. It might take the form of a combined local and national tax, to be levied by each local authority for the national government as well as for itself. The local rate of tax would be decided by each local authority for its locality, and the national rate would be decided by the national government for the country as a whole. A certain percentage of the proceeds from the national component of the combined tax would be redistributed by the national government back to local authorities on a per capita basis, i.e. according to the number of people living in their locality. The defining characteristics of this whole arrangement, and the rights and obligations of local and national governments under it, might have to be laid down constitutionally, to avoid the risk of undesirable controversy every year between national government and local authorities about how it was supposed to work.

The first priority is a study to establish the feasibility of this approach in broad outline. The next stage will be to propose a timetable for phasing in the combined local and national tax on the site value of land and for phasing out the taxes which it is to replace.

International Taxation

The following are among the issues to do with international taxation that need to be dealt with in the 1990s.

The tax harmonization policies and processes of the European Community may either hinder or help Britain and other European countries to develop enabling and conserving systems of taxation. It will be necessary to build up a co-operative network of people in all the European countries who are working to bring in such tax systems, and to make co-ordinated use of their political and pressure-group support.

If national governments are to levy taxes on energy, resources and pollution, they will have to levy corresponding taxes on the energy, resources and pollution content of foreign goods imported from countries which have no similar taxes. How this will be best done, what administrative problems will have to be resolved, what negotiations with other countries and international organizations will be needed, and how much additional revenue these special import taxes will be likely to raise, are matters that must be worked out. In the first instance, they should be part of the feasibility study on the proposed energy tax.

So far as international taxes are concerned, a number of possibilities need to be worked through. These include the proposed taxes on international trading and international currency transfers (Chapter 7). They also include taxes on the extraction of global resources from the sea-bed and Antarctica, as proposed in the Brandt Report of 1980,[6] and on international pollution. Study is needed on which of these taxes should support the international public expenditure of the U.N. and other agencies, and which should be paid into an international development fund to promote self-reliant development in Third World countries (Chapter 7).

Taxes by Design

Existing taxes have not been designed as a system which will encourage people to be economically and socially productive. Nor do they encourage efficient use of resources. They are not enabling or conserving.

There are two priorities for the early 1990s.

The first is to secure widespread national and international support for a new understanding of the functions of taxation, and a new approach to it. This will involve shifting the burden of taxation from useful human work to the occupation of land and the use of energy and resources. It should remove the present tax bias against informal economic activity. At the international and national levels it should encourage self-reliant national and local economic development and redistribute financial resources from richer to poorer countries and from richer to poorer localities.

The second of these two priorities is to carry out proper feasibility studies on the scope for replacing existing taxes with:

* a combined national and local tax on the site value of land;
* a national tax on energy at source;
* pollution taxes;

and for introducing:

* international taxes on imports and currency transfers, and on the extraction of global resources.

Notes and References

1. James Robertson, *Reform Of British Central Government*, Chatto and Windus/Charles Knight, 1971, p. 124.
2. *Future Work*, pp. 174–177, and *The Living Economy*, pp. 189–192.
3. Institute for European Environmental Policy (European Cultural Foundation), Aloys Schulte Str. 6, D-5300 Bonn, Federal Republic of Germany.
4. Farel Bradbury (Hydatum, P.O. Box 4, Ross-on-Wye HR9 6EB, England) has developed his approach to energy taxation over a period of years, in papers on "Resource Economics", "Tax Distribution In the Energy Economy", and "The Joules Of Wealth". His ideas merit detailed research back-up, which has not been available hitherto.
5. See *The Living Economy*, p. 231.
6. *North-South*, Report of the Independent Commission on International Development Issues under the Chairmanship of Willy Brandt, Pan, 1980.

Some of the proposals in this chapter were circulated in early 1987 as a basis for a research project for the New Economics Foundation. It was not possible to take the project forward at that time, but I benefited from constructive comments from, among other, Farel Bradbury, Roy Cattran, David Chapman, Peter Fellgett, Mayer Hillman, John Pezzey, and Malcolm Slesser.

11

Incomes and Capital

Key features of an enabling and conserving economy will, as suggested in Chapter 4, be to do with the distribution of incomes and capital.

For many people, perhaps most, the central aspect of dependence in modern economic life, and the source of the dependency culture which modern economic life has created, is dependence on getting an income either from an employer or from the state. Although the modern industrial state accepts that all its citizens should receive a basic income in one or other of these ways, the actual arrangements for distributing incomes restrict the economic freedom of many, perhaps most, employees and claimants and make them feel dependent.

Because the need for an adequate money income has loomed so large and immediate in most people's lives, those supporting or representing the interests of employees and claimants, such as the trades unions and the pressure groups and campaigning organizations of the poverty lobby, have concentrated mainly on trying to improve the level of incomes under existing arrangements. They have not been able to pay as much attention to the possibility of replacing the existing arrangements, under which paid employment is regarded as the norm and those receiving state benefits are treated as second-class exceptions, with new arrangements that would be less discriminatory, dependency-creating and disabling. Nor have they been able to pay much attention to the possibility that wider distribution of capital could help to solve the problem of low incomes.

So it is helpful to remind ourselves yet again how people originally come to depend on a money income from an employer or the state. This starts when modern economic development deprives people of the capital resources they have previously enjoyed, and hands those capital resources over to people stronger and richer than themselves. This happened in past centuries in what we now call the industrialized countries, when the enclosures of land deprived "the common people" of their capital, that is the wherewithal—the means of production—to supply their own food, to build their own homes, and otherwise to support themselves and their families in a mainly subsistence way of life. From having enjoyed a considerable degree of economic self-reliance, they were turned into paid labourers. The same thing is happening now in other parts of the world—to the arctic peoples being deprived of their means of livelihood by the pipeline operations of oil and gas companies, to the equatorial forest peoples being deprived of theirs by multinational loggers and ranchers, and to Asian and African peasants being deprived of theirs by big dams and other development projects sponsored by national governments and the World Bank.

In working towards a new distribution of incomes and capital, therefore, those of us who live in highly monetarized economies need to keep in mind, not only the very close connection between financial capital and financial income, but also the importance of real non-financial capital and real non-financial income. By real non-financial capital I mean land and houses and equipment and other physical assets which enable people either to earn financial incomes or save financial costs, or both. By real non-financial income I mean the benefits created by informal economic activity, including food and other necessities of life which people—or their families, friends and neighbours—produce directly for their own use.

That non-financial capital and income can, indeed, be just as real as financial capital and income, and that financial security need not be the only basis for real security, was clearly put by Bertram Pokiak and Pierre Tlokka, two native people from Northern Canada, when giving evidence to a public enquiry some years ago:

> Just like you white people working for wages and you have money in the bank, well my bank was here, all around. . . . Whatever kind of food I wanted, if I wanted caribou I'd go up in the mountains. In the delta I get mink, muskrat. But I never make a big trapper. I just get enough for my own use the coming year. Next year the animals are going to be there anyway, that's my bank.

And:

> The white people, they always have some money in the bank. I will never have any money in the bank. The only banking I could do is something that is stored in the bush and live off it. That's my bank. That's my saving account right there.[1]

A Basic Income Scheme

Under the proposed Basic Income Scheme every citizen would receive a basic weekly income from the state unconditionally as of right. This would not be taxed. It would replace the complex existing system of benefits and tax allowances, and it would include the existing state pension.

This idea is supported by people from every part of the political spectrum. It would have many advantages. Unemployment, as a practical administrative status, would be abolished and with it the division of citizens into two classes, employed and unemployed. The poverty trap—which now operates by withdrawing benefits from people when they begin to earn money for themselves —would be abolished, and many useful activities that now fall into the black economy would be legitimized. The unconditional basic income would enable many homeworkers and voluntary workers to do unpaid caring and family work and to undertake many kinds of unpaid productive work in the informal economy. It would make possible a freer market in labour and thus contribute to business competitiveness, since employees would no longer be dependent on their jobs to provide their basic income. Some wages and salaries would no doubt fall as a result. But, at the same time, since poorer workers would become less dependent on unpleasant, menial work for their living, employers would probably have to increase the wages paid for such work. It might then be possible to reverse the present paradoxical situation in which well-off people get highly paid for doing pleasant, interesting work and badly-off people get poorly paid for doing disagreeable but essential work.[2]

Much detailed work has already been done on the practicalities of this idea, such as how high the level of the universal, unconditional basic income would be set, and how it would be funded—what taxes would have to be raised to provide the money for it. Outstanding in Britain has been the work of the late Conservative Member of Parliament, Sir Brandon Rhys Williams, and his research assistant, Hermione Parker.[3] A Basic Income Research Group (BIRG) now exists in the UK, affiliated to a Basic Income European Network (BIEN).[4]

However, as yet no consensus has been reached on the feasibility of the scheme. The general assumption has been that the basic income would be financed out of income tax (applied to all incomes additional to the basic income), or out of value added tax, or out of a mixture of the two. But calculations seem to show that, if a full basic income were to be financed that way, income tax might rise to a level that would discourage people from taking paid work, and the regressive effect of VAT—the tax burden it would place upon poor people contrasted with rich people—might become too great. Other sources of finance, including the land and energy taxes proposed in Chapter 10, will need to be considered.

Lying behind the discussion about practicalities, people tend either to support or oppose the idea of an unconditional basic income according to the view they take of human nature. Supporters, including myself, tend to welcome the idea on the grounds that many people are now prevented from taking up socially useful and personally rewarding work, because under today's arrangements they can't afford to give up an existing job, however valueless they may feel it to be, or—if they are unemployed—to risk losing their eligibility for benefits. We argue that the Basic Income Scheme would liberate such people to do useful work. Opponents argue that, on the contrary, if everyone received an unconditional basic income, many people would relax into irresponsible idleness. The right of every citizen to an income would not be matched by an obligation to make any positive contribution to the economic life of society.

That this difference of opinion cannot straightforwardly be resolved is partly due to the fact that economic life is no longer, since the middle ages, based primarily on the idea of mutual rights and obligations. That raises a general issue for the twenty-first-century economic order that needs to be explored further—see Chapter 3. However, the more immediate need is for further study of the feasibility of financing a full basic income, taking account—as previous research has not—of revenue that may be expected from the land and energy taxes proposed in Chapter 10.

This study of the feasibility of financing a full Basic Income Scheme will also have to take into account—again as previous research has not—the possible effects of wider capital ownership on people's incomes and income needs. Financial capital brings in unearned income; home ownership brings in a saving of expenditure on rent; and ownership of means of production enables people to earn income from their work, or to reduce their personal and household expenditure by providing some of the necessities of life for themselves, or a bit of both. In other words, the level of income that a Basic Income Scheme will have to provide can be reduced by companion measures that result in a wider distribution of capital.

Citizen Capitalists

David Howell, in his important book *Blind Victory*, grasps very firmly the connection between capital ownership and incomes, though he is specifically concerned with policies to free up the labour market and not necessarily with the introduction of a Basic Income Scheme as one of those policies. He says, "The missing half of the proposition, from which talk of more flexible wages should never be disconnected, is that in a liberal and decentralised society . . . support for a decent living standard must be expected to come not just from wages but from capital sources as well. The opening up and vigorous development of these capital sources, as a vital additional prop to family living standards, is just as much part of the necessary labour market reform as are all the other proposals for increased wage flexibility and for lifting the burdens that prevent the labour market working." The title of the chapter from which that quotation comes is

"Wider Ownership: The Absolutely Central Goal". In it Howell argues powerfully that wider ownership is "not just another piece of anti-socialist and anti-collectivist rhetoric, but the key to the solution to the Keynesian dilemma, the successor idea to the Keynesian economic and political order".[5]

Ownership by individuals can be widened in a number of different ways. These include:

* enabling more people to build up their own self-employed businesses;
* encouraging wider share ownership, by enabling more employees to own shares in the companies which employ them, and by enabling more citizens to own shares in privatized nationalized industries;
* enabling more people to build up their own personal pension schemes and their own financial savings;
* enabling more people to own their own houses; and
* making it easier for more people to own their own land.

In Britain in the nineteen-eighties the Conservative government under Mrs Thatcher has subscribed to all of these ideas except the last, at least in rhetoric and theory. But the actual results have been rather disappointing. There certainly has been an increase in the number of people setting up their own businesses, but it is too early to say how permanent and deep-rooted a change this will prove to be. Some more individuals do now own shares, but in practice privatization has been not so much about creating a nation of citizen capitalists as about raising finance for the Exchequer—and transmuting the power of nationalized industry managers and Whitehall civil servants into power and wealth for the Conservatives' friends and supporters in the City. The net result of privatization may have been to put the clock back, by strengthening the impression in most people's minds that shareholding is more to do with speculation and windfall gains for the undeserving than with achieving greater economic independence and security for all. Some progress has been made on personal pension plans and personal equity plans, but not of a fundamental kind. So far as housing is concerned, ownership has certainly grown with the transfer of council houses into private hands, but at the same time the escalating cost of houses has actually made it more difficult for many people, especially young people, to buy their own houses. And, as for a nation of citizen land-owners, that idea has never even figured in the rhetoric of the Thatcher government.

The fact is, I fear, that—with honourable exceptions like David Howell—a majority of Conservatives have looked at these questions through the eyes of an employing and shareholding class on the top half of a ladder whose lower rungs are occupied by wage-earning employees. They have been unable to imagine a future society of equal citizens or a future economic structure not taking the form of a hierarchical ladder of that kind. They have perceived the class division between those who have capital and those who don't as a permanent feature of society. The exploitative, authoritarian and censorious streak in Conservative psychology has welcomed greater flexibility in the labour market, not as part of an enabling package which will enlarge the economic freedom of people now dependent on wage-work, but as an instrument for reducing their independence and teaching them to behave. The typical Conservatives of the nineteen-eighties have not wanted to get rid of the ladder. Nor have they wanted wage-workers to join them on its higher rungs. God forbid! They have wanted to keep them more firmly down on the lower rungs where they belong!

In Britain, then, a key taks for the early nineteen-nineties is to establish in the public mind that, in spite of the false start made in the eighties, wider ownership must be a central feature of the twenty-first-century economy. Many more citizens than today should then enjoy a right to the personal ownership of productive capital assets, financial and non-financial.

In order to get this firmly established, it will be necessary to show what is already happening as regards self-employed business development, wider share ownership both by employees and by the more general public, personal pensions and personal savings plans, ownership of housing, and ownership of land. It will also be necessary to show people how further progress in these respects can be encouraged. Very many specific schemes and ideas need to be brought together and documented in the context of wider capital ownership, ranging from ESOPs (employee stock ownership plans) and GSOPs (general stock ownership plans) through Industrial Common Ownership, to sweat-equity projects for self-build housing.[6]

It may, however, turn out that the most powerful encouragement for wider capital ownership will come from the ripple effects of the tax proposals in Chapter 10. Removing taxes on incomes and capital will make every kind of financial saving simpler and more attractive for many people. Removing tax allowances will reduce the incentives for rich individuals and companies to bid up the price of houses and land. The tax on land will further tend to reduce the attractiveness of land and houses as speculative assets for people and organizations who do not intend to make full use of them. House ownership and land ownership should then become more accessible for many people who are priced out of the housing and land markets today. But we cannot settle these questions without proper study and documentation. This is needed urgently. We need to be able to show in sufficient detail what changes in the distribution of capital, as well as in the distribution of incomes, the tax changes proposed in Chapter 10 could be expected to bring about.

Co-operative Capitalists, Self-Reliant Socialists

Wider ownership will involve spreading the ownership of capital assets more widely not only among individual people, but also among groups of people co-operatively. Although individual capital ownership goes with conventional right-wing ideology and co-operative capital ownership with conventional left-wing ideology, in practice the two often shade into each other. For example, a co-operatively developed residential community may enable its householders to build up an equity stake in their own homes, when on their own they might have found this difficult.

There is very great scope for the further expansion of co-operative capitalism in the spheres of:

* enterprise (producer and consumer co-operatives);
* housing (housing co-operatives and housing associations controlled by the residents);
* land (co-operative and community land trusts, in which ownership and control of the piece of land in question is owned and controlled co-operatively either by those living on it or by the local community as a whole);
* savings and finance (credit unions and other forms of co-operative and mutual savings and investment funds).

There is now a good deal of practical experience about how these forms of co-operative capitalism or self-reliant socialism can be made to work.[7] The need now is to make this knowhow more widely available as a starting point for other people. Apart from the special managerial, technical, marketing and accountancy skills needed for enterprises of this kind, which I shall mention again in a moment, what is wanted first and foremost is a ready made constitutional framework for co-operative enterprise and co-operative capital ownership in connection with any sphere of economic or social activity. It must combine scope for personal initiative with necessary collective safeguards. For example, members of a co-operative should, if possible, have scope to build up a personal capital stake in the enterprise which they will be able to realize if for any reason they decide to move on. But this must be arranged in a way that does not risk the enterprise as a whole coming under the control of a minority of participants or becoming vulnerable to takeover from outside.

Another need is for public policies which will encourage a more favourable institutional climate for self-reliant socialist or co-operative capitalist developments. Public spending programmes which—as recommended in Chapter

8—rely on the third sector, and not just the conventional government and commercial sectors, can make a big contribution here. More specifically, very few lawyers, accountants and bankers, and comparatively few business managers and technical and marketing people in any country in the world are yet familiar with the requirements of the third sector. There is a vital skill shortage to be remedied here as a pump-priming exercise, until a market for these skills, large enough to be self-sustaining, has built up.

New Financial Institutions

One way of helping to widen capital ownership is to make investment capital more easily accessible to larger numbers of people. And that brings us directly to one way in which financial institutions will have to adapt to twenty-first-century needs.

As the numbers of citizen capitalists and co-operative capitalists grow, access to investment capital will, of course, tend to widen automatically. Members of credit unions and other mutual savings institutions will have access to their own savings. Others will be better able than now to provide, either personally or co-operatively, the collateral needed to borrow investment money from existing banks and building societies and other financial institutions. But new financial services and new types of financial institution, such as community banks and local investment funds geared to twenty-first-century values and demand, will also be needed to support the spread of citizen and co-operative capitalism. As capital ownership widens, this will itself create a self-sustaining market for these new financial services and institutions. But for the near future, again as a pump-priming exercise, special encouragement should be given to new initiatives in this field.

Why should special encouragement be necessary? Well, we all know why "most bankers dwell in marble halls". It is

> because they all observe one rule
>   which woe betide the banker who fails to heed it,
> which is you must never lend any money to anybody
>   unless they don't need it.

Ogden Nash was being funny, but the underlying truth is all too serious. Conventional financial institutions are biased, as is the conventional economic system which has thrown them up, against a wider distribution of wealth. In fact, they are positively biased towards transferring resources from the poor to the rich, because that is more profitable for them. Third World debt is the most obvious current example of banks transferring resources from poor to rich, but by no means the only one. The national branch banking networks in countries like Britain systematically siphon the savings of people in poor parts of the country into investment in richer and more profitable parts, or channel them—through the international financial markets—to other richer and more profitable parts of the world. According to conventional banking principles this is quite natural and proper. Banks are expected to get the best available return on their money. They would be failing in their commercial duty if they did not do so.

Again, a considerable body of experience and know-how is now available, both from industrialized and Third World countries, about setting up grassroots banking and financial institutions to serve the needs of local people.[8] A priority task for the nineteen-nineties is to make this more widely available. In general, we need to apply to financial institutions the principles proposed in Chapter 8 for all economic organizations. More specifically, we need to establish the idea that one of the prime aims of financial institutions in the enabling economy of the twenty-first century will be to find ways of helping people, either individually or co-operatively, to become owners of capital.

Priority Tasks

A high priority for the early 1990s is to get it widely understood that new approaches to the distribution of both incomes and capital will be important features of the twenty-first-century economy. The two must go together, as closely linked parts of a larger enabling package.

The right to a basic income must be decoupled from an obligation to undertake paid work. A basic income should be paid to every citizen unconditionally, as of right. If, as is necessary, this idea is to reach the agenda for mainstream political discussion and debate in the next few years, urgent further study is needed of how to finance a Basic Income Scheme. This must be closely linked with study of the feasibility of shifting the tax burden off financial income, capital and value added, and on to the occupation of land and the use of energy and resources, as proposed in Chapter 10. It must take into account possibilities for the wider distribution of capital and the effect these would have on income and income needs.

The wider distribution of capital, individually and co-operatively owned, financial and non-financial including land, is of central importance. There is a great deal of relevant experience and research, and many proposals for taking things forward. But hitherto the field has been regarded as of secondary economic importance. It has also been fragmented between widely divergent interest groups, often with opposed right-left political sympathies, such as the wider share ownership movement and the community land trust movement, and the small business movement and the co-operative movement. What is urgently needed now is to bring the pieces together in a non-party-political context. We must establish the scope for wider capital ownership in all its forms as the "successor idea to the Keynesian economic and political order" and a vital feature of the twenty-first-century economy.

These new approaches to the distribution of incomes and capital, together with the need to make investment capital more widely accessible, will call for new financial services and financial institutions. Financial institutions whose function is to enable people who are not already significant owners of capital to build up a position of greater financial self-reliance, individually and co-operatively, will be a new feature of the twenty-first-century economy. The seeds of this development already exist. A priority task for the 1990s is to clarify plans for fostering it.

Notes and References

1. *Northern Frontier, Northern Homeland*, Minister of Supply and Services, Canada, 1977, p. 94. This beautifully produced report of the Mackenzie Valley Pipeline Inquiry by Mr Justice Thomas R. Berger is chock full of insights into an economic way of life based on renewable resources, and of the destructive impact on it of modern industrialized development.

2. Fuller accounts of the arguments for a Basic Income Scheme will be found in Tony Walter, *Basic Income: Freedom from Poverty, Freedom to Work*, Marion Boyars, 1989. Also see index references to "guaranteed basic income" and "basic income" in *Future Work* and *The Living Economy*.

3. See, for example, *Stepping Stones to Independence: National Insurance after 1990*, by Brandon Rhys Williams and edited after his death by Hermione Parker, with a foreword by Rt Hon. David Howell MP, Chairman of the One Nation group of Conservative MPs, and a preface by Professor James Meade; Aberdeen University Press, 1989.

4. The Basic Income Research Group, 102 Pepys Road, London SE14 5SG, publishes a quarterly *BIRG Bulletin* and holds seminars and conferences. The international secretary of the Basic Income European Network (BIEN) is Walter Van Trier, Bosduifstraat 21, 2018 Antwerpen, Belgium.

5. David Howell, *Blind Victory: A Study in Income, Wealth and Power*, Hamish Hamilton, 1986.

6. Some of these are discussed in *Future Work* —see index references to "capital"—and in *The Living Economy*. But neither book, and no other that I know of, puts forward a comprehensive package of practical proposals for a wider distribution of capital in all its forms.

7. Again, references to many examples will be found in *Future Work* and *The*

Living Economy. But a comprehensive approach to the development of co-operative capital ownership in connection with all aspects of economic and social life, still has to be worked up.

8. I gave examples in "The Economics Of Local Recovery" and "Socially Directed Investment: Its Potential Role In Local Development", papers presented to The Other Economic Summit in 1986 and to a New Economics Foundation conference on "Converging Local Initiatives" in 1987 (New Economics Foundation, 88/94 Wentworth Street, London E1 7SE).

12

Whose Money System Is It, Anyway?

How, then, can we make the money system work more fairly and efficiently as a vital part of an enabling and conserving multi-level one-world economy? The short answer is, I suggest, twofold. First, we must look at money in the new way suggested in Chapter 9, thinking of it not so much as a kind of commodity some of which belongs to each one of us, but rather as a system in which we all participate. Second, we must question whether the state and banking monopoly over this system, derived historically from the power of kings to mint coins, is still useful or necessary.

This chapter takes us into this new ground. Earlier chapters have suggested what various economic agents—people and households, local, national and international governments, and other organizations—can do to control the flows of money to them and from them more purposefully. The more democratic and open approach to organizational decision-making of Chapter 8, the tax changes of Chapter 10, and the changes in the distribution of incomes and capital of Chapter 11, can all help to improve the overall fairness and efficiency of how the money system operates. But they will not touch the basic features of the money system itself: what currencies are permitted and how they can be interchanged with one another; how money is brought into existence and made available for use; how credit and debt are created; and what effect interest has on economic life.

What changes are now needed in these respects? These are probably the most difficult, as well as some of the most important, questions that the twenty-first-century economy will have to resolve. It is possible to see how to start on the right way forward, but not yet to see what the long-term answers to these questions should be. For that reason, parts of this chapter are rather more theoretical and speculative than some other chapters.

This is partly because so much mystification has grown up around the monetary and financial system. But it is also because of the genuine conceptual complexity of the issues. For example, how are we to establish an objective standard of value, to which—it is still widely assumed—a sound money system must be linked? This seems like a variant of the old problem about the relationship between actual prices and real values that troubled Adam Smith,[1] and the even older and more general problem about the relationship between symbols and reality that has puzzled philosophers for thousands of years. Ultimately, it is a non-problem, in the sense that it has no possible solution. For practical purposes we have to start by recognizing this, and then going on from there. After all, the scoring units in many scoring systems, like goals in football, are not tied to baskets of commodities in the real world. Money is just a scoring system of a particular kind. Why does it have to be any different? But these are clearly not easy questions to unravel.

So this is one of the areas in which genuinely sophisticated analytical study and creative imagination of a logical and mathematical kind, as well as powerful politico-economic advocacy, will be needed in the next few years. This chapter suggests how we might most usefully start.

A Multi-Level Currency System

Earlier chapters have touched on future currency developments—Chapter 5 on the possible role of local currencies in more self-reliant local economies, Chapter 6 on the emergence of a European currency, and Chapter 7 on the need for a world currency. One important task for the early nineteen-nineties will be to encourage the introduction and use of local and international currencies. Another will be to work out how, as these new currencies evolve, a multi-level currency structure—for the multi-level one-world economy of the twenty-first century—would and should work.

We need to start by hypothesizing such a multi-level structure of currencies—a world currency for use in international trading, national currencies for use in national trading, and local currencies for use in local trading, together with regional or continental currencies like the ecu (European currency unit) for use in regional or continental trading. We also need to envisage freedom to exchange currencies, but with a buffering mechanism or threshold between them. This might take the form of the international currency tax on exchanges between one national currency and another suggested in Chapter 7. As local currencies are introduced, comparable taxes at national level on local currency exchange transactions should be considered. These taxes—by helping to make it more costly to pay for imported than home-produced goods and services—will encourage economic self-reliance at national and local levels. We need to imagine what will happen as, in the course of time, some currencies become more desirable than others and appreciate in relative value. We need to simulate the workings of a multi-level currency system on these lines, to see how it might be expected to work and how its workings might be improved.

International currencies and related international monetary developments are already the subject of much economic discussion and debate, and there is no need to add further to what was said about them in Chapters 6 and 7. But a word is needed about local currencies, since they are a much less familiar idea.

The argument in favour of local currencies is, briefly, that when localities depend entirely on national (or supra-national) currencies as the medium of exchange to facilitate local economic activity, declining local competitiveness in the national or international economy may result in too little money being available in local circulation even for internal economic purposes within the locality itself. A situation then develops, as in recent years in many formerly flourishing industrial cities in Europe and North America, when local unemployment rises and local land and other physical assets lie unused, while many local needs remain unmet—all for want of enough money circulating locally as a medium to facilitate local exchange. In terms of Keynesian demand management, the demand management policies appropriate for a national economy at any particular time are likely to be inappropriate for many of the local economies within it. As Jane Jacobs puts it, "Today we take it for granted that the elimination of multitudinous currencies in favor of fewer national or imperial currencies represents economic progress and promotes the stability of economic life. But this conventional belief is still worth questioning . . . National or imperial currencies give faulty and destructive feedback to city economies and this in turn leads to profound structural flaws in those economies, some of which we cannot overcome, however hard we try."[2]

How, then, could a local government authority set about remedying this? How could it put local purchasing power into its local economy? One answer is to do what was done in Worgl in Austria in the 1930s, as David Weston has described.[3] The burgomaster of Worgl issued local currency in the form of "tickets for services rendered". They were used for paying wages to men employed on public works, who would otherwise have been unemployed. During the first month of issue these tickets are said to have circulated twenty times as a form of local currency. Taxes were paid, unemployment was reduced, and local shopkeepers prospered. Mayors of two hundred other Austrian towns decided to follow suit. But the Austrian National Bank took legal action against the experiment, the Austrian Supreme Court decided in favour of the Bank, and the innovation was squashed.

Various possibilities of this kind need to be tried out as experimental pilot projects, and studies and simulations need to be made of the likely local and national consequences of local currencies or quasi-currencies becoming a regular feature of the twenty-first-century economy. Possibilities include the issue by local authorities of IOUs—as at Worgl—in payment of local wages and salaries and purchases of all kinds, or as bonds in exchange for loans. These IOUs and bonds would be subsequently acceptable at a premium (or perhaps be made obligatory) as tax payments and other payments to the local authority itself. The expectation would be that, between being issued by and being paid back to the local authority, they would circulate in the local economy as a medium of exchange, a store of value and a unit of account. Local banks and other financial institutions would soon learn to handle accounts for their customers denominated in local currency units, alongside accounts denominated in the national currency.

Arrangements would be needed for enabling people to exchange these local currencies with other local currencies and the national currency, just as national currencies are now exchanged with one another through banks and other foreign exchange businesses. The feasibility of taxing exchange transactions involving local currencies is one of the aspects that needs to be studied. The proceeds of this tax could be redistributed to local authorities on a per capita basis—see Chapter 5.

Deregulated Currencies

In evolving an appropriate money system for the twenty-first-century economy, we should not necessarily assume that government authorities, whether local, national or international, should be solely responsible for it. Another important subject for study is the role to be played—as the twenty-first-century economy evolves—by commercial companies and non-commercial groups, and even perhaps by individuals, issuing their own money.

"Our monetary and banking system is the product of harmful restrictions imposed by governments to increase their powers. They are certainly not institutions of which it can be said they have been tried and found good, since the people were not allowed to try any alternative."[4] In support of a free money movement comparable to the free trade movement of the nineteenth century, Professor F.A. Hayek has argued that the government monopoly of money has been the cause of four major defects—inflation, financial instability, undisciplined public expenditure and economic nationalism. He has proposed the denationalization of money. The government monopoly should be replaced by competition in currency supplied by private issuers who, to preserve public confidence, will limit the quantity of the money they issue in order to maintain its value.

Hayek has also suggested that "it will be through the credit card rather than through any kind of circulating token money that the government monopoly of the issue of money will ultimately be broken".[5] The significance of electronic and plastic money has now begun to make itself fully felt, with credit cards and cash cards becoming accepted as a feature of economic life. The practical feasibility of proposals like Hayek's for denationalizing money now needs to be established in the light of our new understanding of money. That is of money, not primarily as paper or metal items which physically circulate, but as a scoring arrangement made up of a system of accounts, in which the provision of metal and paper tokens that can be physically transferred from payer to payee is becoming a secondary feature—to facilitate particular types of transaction, especially those that are occasional and small.

The feasibility of commercial currencies must be examined now in the context of a single one-world system in which, although the accounts are denominated in various different units (or currencies), it is possible to arrange for transfers to be made from more or less any account in the world to more or less any other—if sometimes in rather complicated ways and on complicated bases of calculation when unfamiliar currencies are involved in the transaction.

It is not just commercial banks and other commercial businesses that could be permitted or encouraged to issue their own means of payment. Currency innovations can be and have been initiated by local community groups. The Green Dollar Exchange and the LET system (local exchange trading system) on the west coast of Canada are two variants on the idea of an independent system of mutually balancing accounts, whose members issue and manage the "money" used within the system in the form of claims on themselves.[6] Every member has an account held in a central place which keeps the score, as in a conventional current account banking system. Every new account starts at zero, and as members agree transactions with one another they tell the central office to debit and credit their respective accounts with the agreed number of units. The system as a whole is always exactly balanced, with the total debits of the members in debt being exactly matched by the total credits of those in credit. Any group of people can set up a system of this kind. The relevant modern technology is a home computer and telephones, but pen and paper could do almost equally well.

A somewhat different type of experiment with a local currency has been launched in the Berkshire area of Massachusetts in the United States. This has been done in connection with a Self-Help Association for a Regional Economy (SHARE), the aim of which is to enable people in that rural area to invest in small projects which will contribute to local economic self-reliance. Following the thinking of Ralph Borsodi, this new currency (called Berkshares) is denominated in units of a basic local commodity— cordwood. It is indexed against the dollar according to the current dollar price of cordwood, and—not being subject to inflation—is expected to maintain its value better than the national currency. A local bank handles currency exchanges between Berkshares and dollars very simply, as deposits into and withdrawals from two accounts—one in Berkshares and the other in dollars—which SHARE has opened for that purpose.[7]

Self-initiated local exchange systems of these kinds can be seen either as a way of facilitating multilateral barter among local groups for whom money is in short supply, or as a way of providing an alternative form of money. In practice these come to the same thing. It would be unrealistic to exaggerate the impact which these experiments with new local currencies and related forms of self-financing for small-scale economic activities have made so far; or to forget that, because they still have to swim against the prevailing tide, they meet with many practical difficulties. But they do suggest that, along with other local financial innovations like local investment funds, local government bonds, and so on, local currencies and quasi-currencies could have a significant role as an aspect of local self-reliance. They also help to make it clear how, in insisting on retaining the old kingly monopoly over the provision of money (or, as we now need to think of it, the provision of a monetary exchange system), national governments and national banks have kept people and places economically dependent. Monopoly control of the money system is the most basic impediment to greater economic self-reliance.

Debt, Interest and Credit

We come now to some of the most difficult questions of all, the questions of debt and interest and the creation of credit.

The conventional approach to these, which most people have had to take more or less for granted, is based on the assumption that money is a substantive thing divided into substantive units, each of which belongs to some particular person or organization. There is my money and your money and their money. If it is my money, it cannot be yours or theirs. If you do not have enough money for your immediate purposes and I have money which I do not need for mine, it makes sense for you to borrow or hire my money, just as you might borrow or hire my car. If you borrow or hire my money, it makes sense for you to pay me a hiring fee, i.e. interest, just as you might pay a hiring fee for my car. (And, when—as happened recently to me—you buy a pair of shoes and arrive home with a box containing two left feet of different sizes, it makes sense to insist that you want your money back!)

This notion of money as something which is yours or mine or someone else's is perfectly understandable, given its historical origins and the way the monetary, banking and financial system has developed. Most people find it difficult to think of money in any other way. But it creates severe problems, which not only cause social injustice and economic instability but are now contributing to the prospect of planetary disaster.

The practice of hiring out money not in immediate use and taking interest on it is at the heart of the monetary and financial system as it functions today. Anyone or any organization that has money to spare from time to time—i.e. has a positive score—is expected to hire it out at interest, and anyone or any organization that needs to borrow someone else's score from time to time is expected to pay interest on it. As both American and German scholars have shown in recent pamphlets, the all-pervasive effect of interest throughout the workings of the system has led, as it was bound to lead, to exponential growth in total outstanding debt and in the flow of interest payments required to service it.[8] This need to pay continually growing interest on the continually growing burden of debt throughout the world economy deepens the economic dependency of many debtors and pushes them into ecologically damaging economic activities. An all too obvious example of this is the Third World debt crisis.

The continuing growth of total debt and its continually growing impact on economic life has its root cause in the fact that, under the present system, all new money which is created and put into circulation starts off in the form of an interest-bearing debt. The way it happens is this. A bank makes a loan to a customer in the form of a book entry, without having to borrow the money from anyone else and take it out of circulation that way. On receiving the loan, the customer may leave the money in a bank account, or pay it to someone else who puts it in their bank account, or cash it for banknotes. Whichever of these things happens, new money has been brought into circulation. The money supply has been increased. Meanwhile, the customer will be paying the bank regular sums of money as interest on the debt until it is paid off. This way the banks, in effect, create new money out of thin air, and they and their shareholders, managers and employees get the benefit of the interest which their customers pay on it.

The pervasive role of interest in the economic system results in the systematic transfer of money from those who have less to those who have more. Again, this transfer of resources from poor to rich has been made shockingly clear by the Third World debt crisis. But it applies universally. It is partly because those who have more money to lend, get more in interest than those who have less; it is partly because those who have less, often have to borrow more; and it is partly because the cost of interest repayments now forms a substantial element in the cost of all goods and services, and the cost of necessary goods and services looms much larger in the finances of the poor than of the rich. Calculations made recently in West Germany taking these various factors into account show that, dividing all households into ten groups of 2.5 million in order of household wealth, the net effect of interest payments is a significant transfer of wealth to the two richest groups from the rest.[9]

This systematic transfer of money from those who need it most to those who need it least is one of the factors pushing the world towards catastrophe. It fuels the urge of the very rich, including the huge industrial and financial corporations of multinational business, to compete with one another purely for the sake of economic wealth and power. It lulls the moderately well-off into a complacent sense that all is well with economic life. For those still clambering up the ladder of economic achievement, it seems to confirm—falsely—that an enterprise culture is essentially a money-grubbing culture. And, by artificially increasing the financial pressures on the less well-off and the poor, it deepens their economic dependency. In each of these ways it stimulates an unnecessarily high level of economic activity and the ecological damage which results.

In Chapter 9 I suggested that we now need to start thinking of money, not as a quantity of things (pounds or yen or dollars) belonging to different owners, but as an accounting system. Its capacity to function effectively depends on its being collectively used by all its users. Its functions are to indicate people's entitlements and obligations in relation to one another and to facilitate economic transactions between them. For philosophers of science and students of the evolution of ideas this change of perception about the nature of money is just one aspect of a wider shift of conceptual emphasis away from things and on to relationships and systems of interaction. The same shift is taking place in sub-atomic physics and the ecological and systems sciences.

When we look at the money system that way and when we begin to think about how it should be redesigned to carry out its functions fairly and efficiently as part of an enabling and conserving economy, the arguments for an interest-free, inflation-free money system for the twenty-first-century economy seem to be very strong. However, I have only recently come to accept this myself and I recognize that, for at least a year or two more, most people will assume—as I have done hitherto—that the idea is a non-starter. Although I suspect that many savers would be quite happy with no interest, provided the system was also inflation-free and the value of their savings was secure, and although it seems clear that the present interest-ridden system is taking us to disaster, no-one has yet studied in any depth how an interest-free, inflation-free money and finance system would actually work.

Many questions arise. Some are to do with how an interest-free economy would operate. What would people do with their unused money? How would they decide who to lend it to? Where would they put their savings? How would people and businesses raise loan capital? What would be the effect on equity capital? What would governments use instead of interest-rate policies? How would a prohibition on paying and taking interest payments be enforced? Might it be possible to prohibit interest on legally recoverable loans made in recorded account-based transactions, while allowing interest payments on loans which, having been made in unrecorded cash transactions, would not be recoverable at law?[10] And so on. Other questions are about the transition, or conversion, from today's economy to an interest-free economy. How would an interest-free economy be phased in? How would existing interest-bearing debts be phased out? Who would benefit and who would suffer, if it were done one way rather than another? Could it be done piecemeal? Coult it be done by one country unilaterally?

As I say, virtually no serious work has yet been done on these questions anywhere in the world. It is a top priority to start.

Financial Collapse or Soft Landing?

Some kind of world-wide financial breakdown will almost certainly occur before the end of the century. We must try to avert this. But, if and when it does happen, we must be ready for it—not like conventional financial experts, in order to profit from it for ourselves and our clients, but so that we know how the money and finance system should be reconstructed afterwards. We need to understand why the breakdown will happen and what form it will take.

The essential point is that, in the present situation, financial stability depends on continually rising cash flows to support continually rising capital values and continually rising levels of debt. Rising levels of debt call both for rising cash flows to service them, and for rising capital values to provide security for them. Rising capital values call both for rising cash flows to support them (as return on investment in the assets they represent), and for rising levels of debt to finance them. Rising cash flows call both for rising levels of debt to provide the money for them, and rising capital values to make people feel they have plenty of money to spend. The process is like a whirlwind. It has to keep spiralling upwards in order to keep going at all.

Breakdown occurs when a large enough number of people and organizations (and nations) find they can no longer generate the incoming cash flows (income) to support the outgoing cash flows (expenditure) to service their debts. As more of them try to stay afloat by selling their capital assets, capital values fall. As some of them go bankrupt, they cut off the cash flows on which other people and organizations were depending in their turn to service their debts. They too have to sell capital assets, and capital values fall further. More people go bankrupt. A self-reinforcing downward spiral now takes hold.

Financial breakdowns or slumps of this kind have occurred regularly from time to time in the past. As the upward spiral of rising cash flows, rising debt and rising capital values goes on, it becomes more vulnerable to perturbations. These may take the form of specific events that reduce the flows of income needed to sustain existing capital values and levels of debt. Triggers might include a repudiation of Third World debts, or a slump in worldwide farm prices, or a collapse in stock exchange prices as in October 1987. Whatever specific forms such perturbations take, they are amplified if a general lack of confidence arises from a sense that people and organizations and nations are overborrowed and that capital assets are overvalued.

Even in the normal course of events such a breakdown would be very likely to occur before the end of the century, simply because the financial situation of so many people and organizations and nations all over the world is now so over-extended. The near certainty that a breakdown will occur arises from the new challenge which the world now faces, and with which this book is concerned. That is the urgent need to change the direction of the world's economic development. The fact is that switching away from the present path of development which is dependency-creating and ecologically destructive to one which is enabling and conserving, will result in systematic reductions of cash flows throughout economic life. As the transition to the new development path gathers pace a negative multiplier effect will come into operation.

Take first the enabling aspect. As nations become economically more self-reliant and less dependent on imports and exports, they will become less dependent on outward cash flows associated with imports, and therefore also on inward cash flows associated with exports. In relation to all external economic entities, their cash flows will decline. The same is true for localities within nations. As local economies become more self-reliant, they too will become less dependent on outward and inward cash flows and more reliant on money circulating internally within the locality. Their cash flows, too, will decline in relation to all external economic entities. And the same goes for persons and households. As they become more, not less, economically self-reliant, outward and inward cash flows between them and the economy outside will also tend to decline. Their own capital equipment supported by their own unpaid work will provide them and their families and friends and neighbours with a greater proportion of the goods and services they need. In each case it is apparent that an enabling economy will be a cost-saving economy. And a cost-saving economy is one in which people and localities and organizations and nations pay each other less. Cash flows decline.

Now consider the conserving aspect. A conserving economy is also a cost-saving economy. A world society in which the virtue of thrift is systematically practised by billions of people in every department of economic life as regards the use of real resources, will not be one in which the money value of incomes and expenditures and capital assets systematically continues to grow. Quite the reverse. Take agriculture. As conserving methods of farming—less dependent on continuing high inputs of chemical fertilisers and pesticides—become more widespread, both the costs incurred and the income generated by farming a given piece of land with a given number of people will tend to fall. If you try to keep your crops pest-free by applying doses of chemical pesticides, you have to continue buying these pesticides regularly; whereas establishing a population of pesticidal predators in your fields or greenhouses is something you hope to do once for all. Or take energy. So long as your car or your home or your factory is inefficient in energy use, you have to go on regularly spending large sums of money on energy. But once you have an energy-efficient car or home or factory, your outgoings on energy are permanently reduced. Those cash flow reductions—and the countless others like them that would result in an economy orientated to conservation and efficient use of resources—will have a very powerful ripple effect through the whole money-based network of economic activities. Cash flows will decline.

This falling off in the levels of cash flow as we make the transition to an enabling and conserving economy will bring a financial crisis calling for financial retrenchment all round. This will be a serious matter. It calls for urgent contingency planning now.

The falling off in cash flows will also have a devastating effect on economic growth as conventionally measured. This will not matter at all, once it is generally understood that the conventional notion of economic growth is a conceptual nonsense, based only on the aggregate quantity of money being earned and spent, and bearing little relation, if any, to progress in wealth and wellbeing for people and the Earth. But it does underline the need for the development and introduction of new, more intelligent ways of monitoring and measuring genuine progress or deterioration in that regard. I need not say more here about the shortcomings of Gross National Product and other conventional indicators and measures of economic performance. They are already widely understood,[11] and the development of alternative economic indicators will be discussed in depth in a book sponsored by the New Economics Foundation which is to be published in 1990.[12]

Money as Servant

Money, as I said in Chapter 9, now plays the dominating role in late industrial society that religion played in the late middle ages. Like the Church of that earlier time, today's monetary and financial system has grown into a gigantic worldwide system of extortion, employing a large proportion of the most able people in the world, distracting everyone's energies from activities of real value, and distorting people's relationships to society and the natural world. It cannot continue indefinitely to extend its domination. It will break down, perhaps sooner rather than later.

We should not just wait until this happens. We must try to transform the money system—from master into servant. Doing so will be an important part of the transition to an enabling and conserving economy. It means turning money and finance into a system for registering people's entitlements and obligations towards one another, for enabling them to secure their entitlements, and for encouraging them to meet their obligations.

That is the context in which it is now necessary to re-examine afresh the concepts of money as a medium of exchange, a store of value, and a unit of account. For practical purposes, these concepts need to be rephrased as questions, on the following lines: what arrangements are needed, in an enabling and conserving one-world economy, to enable people to exchange goods and services freely and fairly with one another? to enable people to store entitlements for goods and services, and therefore to enjoy a degree of security, for the future? to ensure that the value of such entitlements remains stable over time? How should the existing money and finance system be developed to provide these arrangements?

In this new context—of the monetary and financial system as a scoring system which needs to be re-designed to function properly—it may well prove useful to reformulate the proposals of a number of imaginative earlier thinkers on these issues. F.A. Hayek has been mentioned already. Others earlier this century include Silvio Gesell, who advocated the replacement of interest by a circulation fee, so that money not in use would decline rather than increase in value through accrual of interest; and C.H. Douglas, the founder of social credit. These, and others whose ideas never wholly caught on, still have their followers. In the altogether new situation now arising, their insights—and those of other individuals and groups regarded by the monetary and financial establishment as well beyond the fringe—may help to stimulate valuable new thinking.[13]

As I said at the start of this chapter, these basic questions about money and finance are among the most difficult we face. It is not yet possible to give clear answers to them. But it is possible to see the way forward.

We need to encourage and initiate serious studies on how a multi-level currency system—international, national and local—will work; how commercial and other non-governmental currencies, including quasi-currencies and barter arrangements, will fit into it; what is to be the role of interest and debt; how far, in the first instance, it would be possible for one country—or even one locality or one group of people—to go ahead with these monetary innovations unilaterally, while remaining economically viable in a competitive world; and how, as the transition to an enabling and conserving economy gathers pace, the wind-down of today's financial system can be steered to a soft landing. In parallel with these research studies, we need to interest informed opinion in the subject and bring the issues into the realm of public discussion and debate. Meanwhile, in parallel with this research and debate, we need to press forward at the political and practical level with the introduction of experimental local currencies and quasi-currencies, and with the proposals in other chapters, such as the international financial developments in Chapter 7.

Notes and References

1. I discuss this question in *Future Work* (pp. 89–106), in a chapter on the valuation of work.

2. Jane Jacobs: *Cities And The Wealth Of Nations*, Penguin, 1986 (p. 158).

3. See *The Living Economy* (pp. 196 ff).

4. F.A. Hayek, *Denationalisation of Money*, Institute of Economic Affairs, London, 1978 (p. 128).

5. In Barry Siegel (ed.), *Money In Crisis*, Pacific Institute, San Francisco, 1984, quoted in Thomas H. Greco, *Money and Debt: A Solution to the Global Crisis*, privately published (from P.O. Box 23011, Rochester, N.Y. 14623, U.S.A.), 1989.

6. See *The Living Economy* (pp. 200–203).

7. Information from Robert Swann, E.F. Schumacher Society, Box 76, RD3, Great Barrington, MA 01023, U.S.A.

8. Thomas H. Greco (see Note 5); and Margrit Kennedy, *Interest and Inflation Free Money*, Permaculture Institute Publications (Steyerberg, Federal Republic of Germany), 1988.

9. Margrit Kennedy (see Note 8).

10. The distinction between recorded, account-based monetary transactions and unrecorded, cash-based transactions raises a number of possibilities for the future. In particular, the arguments for and against taxing cash—by charging a premium over and above its face value when issuing it—should be studied.

11. See, for example, index references to GNP in *The Sane Alternative, Future Work* and—especially—*The Living Economy*.

12. Victor Anderson, *Alternative Economic Indicators*, Routledge, 1990 (in prospect). See also Chapter 4, Note 11.

13. Mark Kinney (950 Martinsburg Road, Mount Vernon, Ohio 43050, USA) and his fellow networkers are a good example of where useful new monetary and financial ideas are coming from.

13

Reorientating the Real Economy

How should we set about applying the principles of the new economic order to specific spheres of real economic activity and real life? This chapter briefly outlines the kind of strategic reappraisals needed for: work; technology and industry; energy; food and agriculture; transport, housing and planning; health; information and communication; education, leisure and the arts; and peace, order and security. Also included are a few paragraphs on the links between this paradigm shift in economics and new developments in science, philosophy and religion.

In each of these spheres—and others like them—the principles and the implications of an enabling and conserving economy need to be worked out in a systematic way, in the context of people, places, nations, the world economy, and organizations of all kinds, as set out in Chapters 4 to 8. We should aim to have a set of these reappraisals completed and published before the end of 1992, together with suggested programmes of change for the remaining 1990s. I am not suggesting that this could be done comprehensively by a "new economics" body like the New Economics Foundation. In some fields much of the work may have been done already by individuals or organizations with a special interest in them. Generally it will best be carried out that way—for example, for technology and industry by an organization like E.F. Schumacher's Intermediate Technology Development Group—with whatever advice and encouragement is needed from a more general "new economics" standpoint.

In each case a broadly comparable approach will be called for. First, as background to working out how the prevailing character of development can now become enabling and conserving, a historical account will be helpful of why and how, in each particular field, it has come to be dependency-creating and ecologically destructive. Ways should then be explored of either internalizing costs which are now externalized or of eliminating them altogether. For example, how can the costs arising from the pollution of river water by chemical farming either be eliminated or be made to fall on the farmers and chemical companies responsible, rather than on the water authorities and consumers as at present? Next, the secondary nature of the conventional political controversies which now dominate public and political discussion should be clearly brought out. In most cases, they simply distract attention from the real underlying issues. For example, the conventional political dispute has been about whether it is better to be dependent on coal or nuclear power in centralized power stations. But it is now coming to be realized that the top priority is to bring in energy conservation and decentralized forms of energy supply. Finally, in every case, it will be necessary to draw up conversion strategies. These should identify obstacles to be surmounted, people who will suffer from the change of direction, ways of easing the transition for them, other steps to be taken, and progress hoped for year by year. Projected progress should be quantified whenever possible, e.g. for reductions to be achieved in total energy demand and the proportion of it to be met from decentralized sources of renewable energy supply.

The following sections briefly sketch some of the ground that some of these reappraisals might cover. They do not aim to be in any way comprehensive, but merely to give some impressions of what will be needed.

Work[1]

History

In ancient society the typical form of work was slavery. In medieval society the typical form of work was serfdom. In industrial society the typical form of work has been employment. In each case the prevailing organization of work has reflected and reinforced a division in society between superiors and inferiors—masters and slaves, lords and serfs, employers and employees. Employment—being dependent on an employer to organize one's work and provide a living income—has been a central feature of the dependency culture of the industrial age.

Enable and Conserve

A central feature of the transition to the new twenty-first century economy must be a transition from employment to a new way of organizing work, fit for free and equal citizens with a stake in the future of human society and the world. Every one should have the right and the responsibility to control their own work. "Ownwork" must take the place of employment as the normal way for people to work. Ownwork will be activity which is purposeful and important, and which people organize and control for themselves. It may be either paid or unpaid. It will be done by people as individuals and as household members; it will be done by groups of people working together; and it will be done by people who live in a particular locality working together locally to meet local needs. For the individual and the household, ownwork may mean self-employment, essential household and family activities, productive leisure activities, and participation in voluntary work. For groups of people ownwork may mean working in a community enterprise, a co-operative, or some other kind of organization in which they have a share of control, or simply working together as partners in social, environmental, scientific or other activities which they value. For localities, the significance of ownwork will be that it contributes to local self-reliance.

Secondary Controversies

The conventional political debate about work centres around how to create employment and what should happen to people who are unemployed. But the more fundamental questions are about how to liberate people from their dependence on employment, and how to enable them to secure a livelihood while working for themselves and one another.

Conversion Strategies

Proposals made in Chapters 4, 5, 6, 8, 10 and 11 about people, places, nations, organizations, taxes, and incomes and capital will all help to bring about the transition from employment to ownwork as the normal way to work. Changes in other spheres, as outlined in the following sections of this chapter, will also help. The task is to bring all these together as a strategy for the future of work and to plan its implementation through the 1990s.

Technology and Industry[2]

History

During the industrial age, technologies and industries have been and still are developed primarily in accordance with the aims of rich and powerful people and organizations competing with one another to increase their wealth and power, using other people and natural resources and environment in order to do so, and able to avoid much of the cost of whatever social and environmental damage they cause. As they have been developed hitherto, technology and industry have thus had an inherent tendency to be dependency-creating and ecologically destructive. This does not call for an anti-technology, anti-industry reaction. It calls for positive development of technology and industry of a different kind.

Enable and Conserve

Instead of continuing to develop new technologies which expand the power of big business and centralized government, we must now positively develop technologies that enable people to control their own work, to meet their own and other people's needs more directly, and to conserve resources and protect the environment.

Internalize Costs

An economy which systematically tends to internalize costs will be characterized by small-scale, decentralized, conserving technologies and industries, owned and controlled by the people who use them and have to live with their impacts. The scale of the externalized social and environmental costs now imposed by the continued development of centralizing technologies and industries that reinforce dependency, waste resources and damage the environment, is not fully appreciated. It calls for authoritative study and critical public debate.

Secondary Controversies

Conventional political debate centres around whether super-scale industries and technologies that are inherently dependency-creating and ecologically damaging should be controlled by the state or commercial business. The important question is different. How can these industries and technologies be scaled down, greened, and brought under the control of the people most directly affected by them?

Conversion Strategies

Many proposals in other chapters and other sections of this chapter will help to bring about the transition to enabling and conserving technologies and industries. The task is to bring them together in a strategy for the future of technology and industry, and to plan its implementation through the 1990s. Two particular points should be noted. An important aspect of the systematic reorientation of government spending programmes called for in Chapter 6 will be a switch of emphasis in government research and development (R. and D.)

programmes towards the development and diffusion of enabling and conserving technologies. And the more open corporate decision-making called for in Chapter 8 should include new "technology choice" procedures. These should be designed to allow the various stakeholders in large companies, together with the public and their elected representatives, to consider not only the possible social and environmental impacts of proposed new technological developments, as is done in conventional technology assessment, but also the positive scope for new enabling and conserving technologies to meet social and environmental needs. The assumption that the essential nature of many technologies unavoidably dictates both a large scale of industrial operation and a trade-off between wealth creation and environmental degradation, must be continually questioned.

Energy[3]

History

The development of energy technology and energy use is an outstanding example of the course taken by the economy and economics during the industrial age. People have become increasingly dependent on huge, monolithic energy supply industries like coal and oil and gas—wasteful, polluting and accident-prone—major contributors to acid rain, oil spills and the greenhouse effect. Meanwhile nuclear power, with its heavy security and policing requirements and its devastating potential for environmental disaster, epitomizes the disabling and ecologically destructive effects of conventional economic and technological progress in every sphere. It has been calculated that, if the sum of money needed to build a nuclear power station were invested in energy conservation and energy efficiency instead, it would save over seven times as much energy as the power station would produce. But, by putting the money into new power stations, not into energy conservation, the big battalions have been able to keep people under their thumb. So that is where it has gone.

Enable and Conserve

Future developments in energy must be reorientated towards energy conservation, energy efficiency, and decentralized methods of energy supply from renewable sources. This will not only achieve desired environmental results. It will also enable people and localities to become more self-reliant in energy.

Internalize Costs

The history of nuclear power caricatures the prevailing failure of large-scale industry to internalize the costs associated with it. Nuclear power stations have had to carry neither the R. and D. costs incurred before they are commissioned nor the costs of decommissioning them when their useful life is over. In Britain it has only been the imminent prospect of commercialization that has begun to bring some of these costs into the reckoning. Studies will almost certainly show that, if all the large-scale energy supply industries were made to carry the costs they now externalize, small-scale decentralized energy supply and energy conservation are much more economic. Such studies, and widespread publicity for their findings, are urgently necessary. They should be replicated for most other industries too.

Secondary Controversies

Should we choose dependency on coal, nuclear energy or oil? On Arthur Scargill, or Walter Marshall, or Esso, Shell, BP and the oil-sheikhs? Should we prefer acid rain, nuclear fall-out, or oil pollution? That is what the conventional political argument has been about. The real questions are about how we can reduce our energy dependency altogether and meet our energy needs ecologically.

Conversion Strategies

Many of the proposals made in various chapters, including the chapter on taxes and also including other sections of this one, will help to encourage the required transition from today's dependence on centralized, wasteful and polluting energy industries to greater self-reliance in energy—based on small-scale energy supply technologies, an increase in energy efficiency, and a reduction in energy-expensive activities and energy-expensive products of all kinds. The task is to bring these various approaches and possibilities together as a strategy for the future of energy, and to plan its implementation through the 1990s.

Food and Agriculture[4]

History

Here again development over the past few hundred years has been away from household and local self-reliance in food towards ever-deepening dependence on industrialized agriculture, industrialized food-processing, and food distribution through supermarket chains. The farming methods, the transport and the packaging this involves are ecologically damaging and wasteful of resources. The food produced this way is subject to many health hazards, including pesticide residues in fruit and vegetables, hormones in meat, and salmonella and other diseases in industrially processed food. The way in which factory-farmed animals are reared, transported and slaughtered is inherently pitiless and inhumane.

Enable and Conserve

The transition to a new way of economic life must include a new approach to agriculture—new ways of producing food. These should enable people in their households and localities to provide more of their own food for themselves. They should involve farming and distribution methods that are efficient in the use of resources and ecologically benign. They should produce food which is healthy and nutritious and tastes good. They should treat animals humanely.

Internalize Costs

Earlier in this chapter I have given an example—the need to ensure that agribusiness farmers and chemical companies shoulder the costs arising from river pollution by chemicals used on farms. So let us take this opportunity to point out an important effect of internalizing costs. When costs hitherto imposed on other people are internalized and brought into account, the measured efficiency or profitability of the activity in question goes down. Nuclear power has been mentioned already. The same applies in farming. If agricultural costs are internalized, it will almost certainly be found that organic is more efficient than chemical farming, even when efficiency is conventionally measured in financial terms. And that raises another question about efficiency. Efficiency in terms of what? There are always different possibilities. In agriculture these include efficiency as measured by financial profit (or turnover or capital employed) in relation to the number of workers employed. They may also include the size of the area farmed in relation to profit, turnover, capital, or labour. But, in an energy-conserving economy, agricultural efficiency might well be measured by the calorific value of the food produced in relation to the calorific value of the energy inputs used to produce it. In short, there are always a number of possible ways of measuring efficiency. The measures chosen will depend on what outcomes, what inputs, and what patterns of activity are considered important. Studies are needed, in the sphere of food and agriculture but also in others, on how to measure efficiency. These should be linked with the study of alternatives to Gross National Product and other conventional measures of economic performance and progress mentioned in Chapters 3 and 12.[5]

Conversion Strategies

Many of the proposals made in other chapters will help to encourage the transition towards more decentralized, less energy-intensive and less polluting food-growing. This will enable many localities and even households to become more self-reliant in the provision of food. Again, the task is to pull all these proposals together into a strategy for the future of food and farming in an enabling and conserving economy, and to plan its implementation through the 1990s.

Transport, Housing and Planning[6]

History

The built environment has developed in accordance with the underlying patterns of economic life. As people and localities have become more dependent on outside employers to provide them with work and outside producers to provide them with goods and services, houses have ceased to be centres of production. Separate zones—residential, industrial, commercial—have grown up in towns and cities, and the transport of people and goods has played an ever-increasing part in economic life. Most people now can no longer build their own houses. With rising property values and the tendency for money to migrate to those who already have it, increasing numbers of people find it difficult to get a house at all. And, as transport becomes increasingly necessary, those who cannot afford it suffer increasing deprivation. The resulting geographical pattern of economic life makes people very dependent. It also wastes resources and damages the environment—witness the British government's announcement in 1989 of a £12 billion scheme to increase road traffic in and around London, at the very time the greenhouse effect was headline news.

Enable and Conserve

The key word is access, as opposed to mobility. Enabling people to have better access will reduce their dependence on mobility—access to work, in and around their own homes and localities; access to local shops and hospitals and schools; access to the resources and skills that will enable more people to plan and build their own homes and communities. This will reduce the waste of resources and environmental blight caused by ever-increasing mobility. It will be a conserving, as well as an enabling, strategy.

Internalize Costs

Critical analyses are needed of the costs imposed by the present geographical structures of economic life, of who meets these costs, and of who benefits. For example, the many hidden costs of locating public sector activities in large cities like London or in other over-developed areas, or of favouring big hospitals, hypermarkets and other transport-dependent facilities against local community hospitals and local corner shops, need to be clearly brought out.

Secondary Controversies

The debate about the relative merits of private and public transport is not altogether beside the point. But it is secondary to the main issue: should we concentrate on continuing to increase mobility? should we not rather give priority to improving accessibility?

Conversion Strategies

Again, many proposals in other chapters—for example on regenerating the household and local economies, and on taxing the use of energy and resources, will encourage the transition to a more accessible, less transport-dependent economy. The task is to pull these all together into a strategy for the future of the built environment in an enabling and conserving economy, and to plan its implementation through the 1990s.

Health[7]

History

People's growing dependence on the medical profession and the pharmaceutical industry means that when people now talk about health they are usually referring to sickness. Health services, health policies and health insurance are really sickness services, sickness policies and sickness insurance. Although economic developments over the last few centuries have markedly improved the health of many people, more people are suffering today than ever before from extreme malnutrition and the diseases it brings. Meanwhile, new health hazards from pollution and man-made accidents are arising on an ever-increasing scale. Conventional economic activities and policies have not been concerned with creating a healthy economy.

Enable and Conserve

A healthy economy will be one in which people are enabled, personally and as communities, to take greater control over their own lives and to create healthier living conditions and environments for themselves and one another. An enabling and conserving economy will be one which frees them from as many as possible of the health-damaging social and environmental hazards and stresses, such as unemployment and pollution, which conventional economic development imposes.

Internalize Costs

All economic activities which impose health risks on other people should be obliged to meet the full costs of whatever health damage they cause and to be fully insured against causing it.

Secondary Controversies

Conventional political debate centres around whether people should be dependent on sickness services provided commercially or by the state. That question is not unimportant. But it should not take priority, as it now does, over the question of how people can be enabled to become positively healthier in a positively healthier society.

Conversion Strategies

Health promotion strategists have acquired insights that are more widely relevant to the conversion of today's economy into a more enabling and conserving one. The need "to make the healthier choice the easier choice", as applied to individuals, policy-makers and business leaders, highlights the wider need to make the more self-reliant (or enabling) and conserving choice the easier choice throughout economic life. The principle of not "blaming the victim" for ill-health imposed by factors outside the victim's control, while at the same time insisting that everyone has an obligation—and a right—to take responsibility for her own health, can be extended to other spheres such as unemployment, poverty and lack of education. The process of converting health-damaging industries like tobacco and alcohol into health-creating ones, will—when once it gets under way—have lessons for conversion in other spheres, such as from military production to peaceful, socially useful production. In short, a health-promoting economy will tend to be an enabling and conserving economy, and vice versa. Many proposals in this and other chapters will have spin-offs for health creation. The task is to pull them all together into a strategy for a healthier economy, and to plan its implementation through the 1990s.

Information and Communication[8]

History

Information and communication technologies have mainly been developed and used by powerful industrial-country organizations in competition with one another, in forms that reinforce the dominance of richer over poorer, and of more powerful over weaker, people and localities and nations and cultures. Thus television and other modern mass media treat people as dependent, passive consumers of information products. But, as was mentioned in Chapter 3, information and communication technologies have an opposite potential too. They can also be developed in forms that enable people and localities and nations to take greater control of their lives and reduce their dependence on organizations and forces outside their control. Thus the telephone and the home computer enable people to participate more actively in information processes.

Enable and Conserve

A vital feature of the transition to the new economy of the twenty-first century—which some see as an "information economy"—will be the purposeful design and development and use of information and communication technologies. They must be doubly purposeful. They must enable people to become more active and autonomous participants in information processes rather than more dependent consumers of information products; and they must help to reduce waste and pollution to a minimum.

Conversion Strategies

It will be a big task to turn around the present thrust of development in this field, dominated as it now is by tycoons like Maxwell and Murdoch and giant multinational corporations like IBM, competing for supremacy with one another. But many of the proposals in this and other chapters will create a growing market for decentralized, participatory and conserving uses of information and communication technology. These provide a starting point for working out a strategy for the future of information and communication, and for planning its implementation through the 1990s.

Education, Leisure and the Arts[9]

History

The thrust of conventional development has brought about a perception of education, leisure and the arts in terms of industrialized production and consumption. Education is understood as an industry, with pupils and students seen as dependent consumers of professionalized education rather than as autonomous learners. The education system treats its pupils and students as an industry treats its materials. Pupils and students enter an education factory—in the shape of a school or a college—in a certain stage of formation, they are processed through a variety of production processes, they are quality-tested by examinations at various stages, and they are finally graded as up to standard for a particular range of employee roles in the adult economy. Meanwhile, leisure too is increasingly understood as an industry, with leisure producers providing all forms of leisure products—holidays, sports events and sports equipment, theme parks, musical events and musical equipment of all kinds, gambling casinos, and much else—which leisure consumers pay for. Even the arts have come to be seen as industries, in which professional arts producers provide arts products—plays, poems, paintings, concerts, sculptures and so forth—for lay arts consumers to consume, and which are valued according to the financial profits they generate and the number of jobs they create.

Enable and Conserve

A new, enabling approach to education, leisure and the arts will be an important aspect of an enabling and conserving economy. Education must enable people to develop themselves and their capacities as autonomous human beings and as active citizens of their communities, rather than as dependent employees and consumers. These capacities must include the capacity to manage their own lives, to contribute to the wellbeing of other people and the local, national and world community, to conserve resources and the environment, and to participate actively in leisure and arts activities—as well as in activities connected with work, health and other important aspects of their lives.

Secondary Controversies

The conventional disputes about whether—or to what extent—education, leisure facilities and the arts in their present forms should be provided and sponsored commercially or by the state, are secondary to the question of what education, leisure and the arts are for. Are they for conditioning people into essentially dependent roles as employees and consumers? Or are they for enabling people to develop themselves as individuals and as active, autonomous citizens of an enabling and conserving society?

Conversion Strategies

An economy pervaded by the principles of enabling and conserving, and characterized by more self-reliant people in more self-reliant households and localities, will require—and also provide the conditions for—the new, decentralized, enabling approach to education, leisure and the arts briefly outlined here. The task, in this as in other spheres, will be to draw up enabling and conserving strategies for the future of education, leisure and the arts, and to plan its implementation through the 1990s.

Peace, Order and Security

History

An economic order that has had no moral underpinning to offset self-interest and competition for dominance, and has systematically transferred wealth and power to the rich and powerful from the poor and weak, has helped to create insecurity between and within nations. Inherent in it has been the need for those with power to channel sizeable resources into a capacity for attack and defence against other nations and into the maintenance of property and order at home. In all the bigger industrialized countries this has created large military/internal-security/industrial complexes. From these in turn have now arisen powerful economic vested interests in the jobs, incomes and profits involved—vested interests which, quite apart from whatever the real needs may be, now generate huge pressures to maintain and increase the scale of activity in this field, including most notably the export of armaments. Just as the economic effort now put into dealing with sickness and into the continuing expansion of medical services and the pharmaceutical industry far overshadows what is put into enabling people to be healthy and to create a healthy environment, so the economic effort that now goes into the armed forces, the security and intelligence services, the police and prisons services, and the weapons and security industries, far overshadows what goes into positively trying to create a peaceful society and a peaceful world. The figures are truly astounding. The cost of a Trident submarine would fund a global five-year child immunization programme against six of the world's killer diseases, preventing a million deaths a year. Two days of world military spending would meet the annual cost of the proposed U.N. Action Plan to halt Third World desertification. Two weeks of it would meet the annual cost of the proposed U.N. Water and Sanitation

Decade. The Worldwatch Institute estimates that today, worldwide, as many as fifty million people may be on the military payroll, either as soldiers or as workers in military industry.[10]

Conversion Strategies

In the international sphere, a key role in converting this economic effort to more constructive purposes will be played by the disarmament process. The new direction of economic development outlined throughout this book will also help to create conditions nationally for more peaceful societies and internationally for a more peaceful world. In addition, however, special attention will have to be given to the conversion of existing jobs and production in these areas to socially and environmentally more useful purposes. The need is to work up a phased programme for this through the 1990s.[11]

Science, Philosophy and Religion

The transition to a new way of economic life and thought will be linked to changes in science, philosophy and religion—as Chapter 3 will have suggested. Clarifying these links will help to smooth the economic transition. It will also help to accelerate changes already beginning to be apparent in science, philosophy and religion themselves.

So far as science and philosophy are concerned, the big changes—as with economics—will be in the questions regarded as important and chosen for attention, in the ways and people by whom the selection of those questions is made, and in the ways and people by whom science and philosophy are actually done. A shift of emphasis is already beginning to take place from knowledge to wisdom, from reductionism to a holistic systems approach, and from quantitative to qualitative understanding.[12] Awareness is growing that today's science is dominated by military and economic considerations, and is culturally biased towards the secularism of the western world.[13]

So far as religion is concerned, the big change needed is to find ways of making the economic teachings of world faiths relevant to economic life as people live it and experience it today. These teachings date from the small agricultural societies of past centuries and millenia. With the partial exception of Christianity, they have had little influence on, and have been little influenced by, the dominant path of economic development of the last few hundred years.[14] In 1986, representatives of world faiths came together in Assisi at the invitation of the WorldWide Fund for Nature (WWF) to explore and celebrate the links between religion and conservation. Could they come together in dialogue through the 1990s about the relevance of their teachings to the prospect of a new economic order for the next millenium?[15]

The task for the next two or three years will be to encourage programmes of study, dialogue and public discussion. The aim must be to clarify and spread understanding of the links between progress towards a new economic order and changes taking place in science, philosophy and religion, and to carry these programmes forward through the rest of the 1990s.

Notes and References

The number of relevant publications and organizations is truly vast. The following are suggested for readers not yet familiar with the ideas covered in this chapter who want to go a little further into them.

1. See *Future Work*. Also Charles Handy, *The Future of Work*, Basil Blackwell, 1984.

2. John Davis and Alan Bollard, *As Though People Mattered: A Prospect for Britain*, Intermediate Technology Publications, 1986—see especially Chapters 4 and 5. Also Mike Cooley, *Architect Or Bee? The Human/Technology Relationship*, Hand and Brain Publications.

3. See my paper and others in *Nuclear or Non-nuclear Futures?* (Centre for Energy Studies, South Bank Polytechnic, Borough Road, London SE1 OAA), the proceedings of a symposium held in April 1987.

4. Joan Dye Gussow, *The Feeding Web: Issues in Nutritional Ecology*, Bull, California 1978, is an excellent introduction to this whole field. Also Frances Moore Lappe and Joseph Collins, *Food First: Beyond the Myth of Scarcity*, Ballantine, New York 1979. The Soil Association (83 Colston Street, Bristol B51 5BB) and the Farm and Food Society (4 Willifield Way, London NW11 7XT) are good sources of information.

5. See Chapter 3, Note 11; and Chapter 12, Note 11.

6. See *Access For All? Technology and Urban Movement*, Council for Science and Society, London, 1986—chiefly authored by transport planner Barry Cooper. John Turner, (Tools For Building Community, 51 St. Mary's Terrace, West Hill, Hastings, East Sussex TN34 3LR) and Peter Elderfield (Building and Social Housing Foundation, Memorial Square, Coalville, Leicestershire LE6 4EU) are good sources of information on decentralized approaches to housing, including self-building and self-planning. The Town and Country Planning Association (17 Carlton House Terrace, London SW1Y 5AS) is a good source of information on a similar approach to the built environment generally.

7. In "Health, Wealth and the New Economics" (available from New Economics Foundation, 88–94 Wentworth Street, London E1 7SE) I reported

on the papers and proceedings dealing with health—and sponsored by the World Health Organization—at The Other Economic Summit in 1985.

8. For a fuller discussion, see "The New Economics of Information" (New Economics Foundation—Note 7 above).

9. Among those active in these fields are: The Human Scale Education Movement, c/o "Resurgence", Ford House, Hartland, Bideford, Devon; and Leisure Consultants, Lint Growis, Foxearth, Sudbury, Suffolk. I valued the opportunity to work with John Lane, of Dartington Hall, Dartington, Totnes, Devon, on the 1988 Dartington conference on "What Future for the Arts?".

10. The figures in this paragraph are taken from the 1989 "State of the World" report from the Worldwatch Institute (Norton, New York 1989).

11. Lessons on conversion can be drawn from the failure of the scheme launched by the Lucas Aerospace Combine Shopstewards Committee from 1975 to 1979—see Hilary Wainwright and Dave Elliott, *The Lucas Plan: A New Trade Unionism in the Making?*, Allison and Busby, 1982. The Worldwatch Institute report at Note 10 above mentions conversion initiatives in the U.S.A.

12. See, for example, Nicholas Maxwell, *From Knowledge to Wisdom: A Revolution in the Aims and Methods of Science*, Basil Blackwell, 1984; and Fritjof Capra, *The Turning Point*, Wildwood House, 1982. Part 2 of *Future Work* relates these changes in worldview to changing perceptions of work.

13. See J.R. Ravetz, *Scientific Knowledge and its Social Problems*, O.U.P., 1971; and Ziauddin Sardar, *Islamic Futures*, Mansell, 1985, and *Information and the Muslim World*, Mansell, 1988.

14. For Christianity see William Charlton, Tatiana Mallinson and Robert Oakeshott, *The Christian Response to Industrial Capitalism*, Sheed and Ward, London 1986. Also many recent publications from the World Council of Churches, Geneva.

15. The Assisi Declarations—messages on Man and Nature from Buddhism, Christianity, Hinduism, Islam and Judaism—were published by WWF on 29th September 1986. With backing from WWF and Christian Aid, the New Economics Foundation is—at the time of writing—exploring with ICOREC (the International Consultancy on Religion, Education and Culture) the economic teachings of the faiths and their points of relevance to a new economics.

14

Agenda for the 1990s

At first sight, an agenda for the 1990s which pulls together everything covered in earlier chapters might seem hopelessly over-ambitious. And so it would be, if I had just thought it all up, and if much of it was not already being done by other people in many parts of the world. Luckily it is not a question of starting from scratch. It is a question of bringing into focus what is happening already, helping one another to put our energies more effectively behind it, and dealing with certain key points standing in the way of faster progress. That is the starting point for this chapter.

Some Key Dates

There is some play of argument whether the third millenium will begin on 1st January 2000 or 1st January 2001. This need not detain us. Provided we respect the fundamental insignificance of these dates to non-Christian cultures, we can expect that in the world as it is today both dates will stimulate worldwide reflection on the past and the future. The period between the two—that is the year 2000 itself—will be a period for reappraisal. The decade leading up to it, the 1990s, will be a period of preparation for that reappraisal. We must make it, among other things, a period of preparation for a new economics for the 21st century.

During the 1990s there will be a number of important dates and historical anniversaries. Examples are shown in the table. Other people are doubtless looking forward to other events and occasions of this kind, and there will be many more as the 1990s unfold. In working up our agenda for the 1990s, we can see these as staging posts en route for the year 2000.

Two of these years will be of special significance.

The first is 1992. That year will be the 500th anniversary of what, with ingrained cultural arrogance, European peoples have been taught to think of as the "discovery" of America by Columbus in 1492. That event marked the

Table. *Some Dates in the 1990s*

1990	*May*	International conference to follow up Brundtland Report. Bergen, Norway.
	Summer	Annual economic summit meeting—in U.S.A.
1991		Centenary of "Rerum Novarum", the first papal encyclical on modern economic issues.
	June	International W.H.O. conference on health and environment, Sweden.
	Summer	Annual economic summit meeting—in Britain.
	?	General election in Britain? Otherwise in 1992.
1992		500th anniversary of Columbus's "discovery" of America.
		20th anniversary of the 1972 Stockholm conference on the environment.
		European Single Market due to be brought in.
	Summer	Annual economic summit meeting—in West Germany.
	November	Presidential election in U.S.A.
1993	*Summer*	Annual economic summit—in Japan.
1994		300th anniversary of Voltaire's birth in 1694—time for a new enlightenment?
		300th anniversary of the Bank of England.
		50th anniversary of Bretton Woods agreement on setting up the I.M.F. and World Bank.
	Summer	Annual economic summit—in Italy.
1995	*Summer*	Annual economic summit—in Canada.
	October	50th anniversary of the United Nations.
	December	50th anniversary of I.M.F. and World Bank.
1966	*Summer*	Annual economic summit—in France.
	November	Presidential election in U.S.A.
1997		Capitalist Hong Kong returns to socialist China.
	Summer	Annual economic summit—in U.S.A.
1998		500th anniversary of Vasco da Gama's voyage to India round the Cape of Good Hope.
	Summer	Annual economic summit—in Britain.
1999	*Summer*	Annual economic summit—in West Germany.

beginning of the aggressive expansion of European Christian and subsequently European secular culture all over the globe. This gave rise to the dominance of today's amoral economic worldview over those of other cultures. It is that which now threatens the very survival of human civilization and even of life on earth. 1992 will thus provide an occasion for a worldwide reappraisal of the present economic order. (The 500th anniversary of Vasco da Gama's voyage to India in 1498 will provide an opportunity for a repeat performance in 1998.) The fact that 1992 will also be the 20th anniversary of the 1972 Stockholm conference on the environment, and the date by which the European Single Market is due to be brought in, will help to attract attention to some of the key issues.

The second particularly significant time for our purposes will be 1994/1995. This will be the 300th anniversary of the Bank of England, the world's first central bank in a modern monetary system. It will be the 50th anniversary of the United Nations and its associated organizations—especially the World Bank and the International Monetary Fund. This will be a time to discuss and debate fundamental reforms in national and international economic institutions.

We may take these two dates as marking the first two stages in the programme of change which we are aiming to mobilize for the 1990s. The first stage should culminate in 1992 with a worldwide reappraisal of the mode of economic development that has been associated with European world domination in the modern age. One of its outcomes will, I hope, be the publication in 1993 of a much firmer and more detailed programme for the remaining 1990s than is possible now. The second stage will culminate in 1995 with clearly specified proposals for reforming today's national and international economic institutions, firmly rooted in the principles of an enabling and conserving, multi-level one-world economy. One of its outcomes, in turn, should be the publication in 1996 of a further updated programme for the remaining 1990s. By that time, incidentally, it is to be hoped that the annual economic summit meetings will provide a more effective and representative forum than they do today for discussing the real economic problems of the world.

Within this outline framework, the following paragraphs suggest a provisional timetable for the early 1990s for carrying forward the tasks identified in previous chapters. This work will need to be done by many different people and organizations of many different kinds in many different countries in a loosely knit network of shared understanding and co-operation. It will be useful if a number of centres around the world with a general interest in "new economics"—like the New Economics Foundation—can facilitate this process in regular communication with one another. It will be useful if some of these new economics centres can acquire the resources needed to sponsor key research studies, conferences and information exchanges that might otherwise not take place. It will be useful if they can stimulate publishers to put out, both for professional and for lay readerships, series of books and pamphlets covering various aspects of an enabling and conserving economy. But the vast bulk of the actual work required will need to be undertaken by people and organizations whose primary interest is in particular areas of economic activity and economic thought—such as the household economy, or purposeful consumerism, or the local economy, or taxation, or currency reform, or energy, or agriculture, or whatever.

Laying the Foundations—Chapters 1 to 3

National and international public awareness and discussion about the need for a new path of development are already building up. The aim should be to ensure that by 1992 the key features of a new economic order are as common a topic for worldwide debate in the public media as environmental issues are today.

An important aspect of this process will be a broadly based international campaign. This should be underpinned by a common framework of understanding and action, evolving out of many different initiatives, including this present book. The drive behind this international campaign will have to come mainly from individual people and non-governmental organizations (NGOs), at least in the early 1990s until governments, businesses and other mainstream organizations can be persuaded to fall in behind it. By 1992, therefore, the aim should be to evolve a degree of consensus among a worldwide network of NGOs concerned with Third World development, the environment, poverty, health, and voluntary activities of many kinds, that they all have an interest in helping to create a new, enabling and conserving, multi-level one-world economic order. More specifically, the aim should be to have them co-operating by 1992 in a range of new economics campaigns and projects, including commissioning a joint annual review of progress towards the new economic order.

Developing the conceptual foundations for this new 21st-century economic order will present a challenge of the first importance to the intellectual and academic world. The economics profession on its own will not be able to meet it. Some of the groundwork needed to put new economic ideas on the academic agenda will probably continue to have to be done outside the academic world and independently of it altogether. But an organized interdisciplinary academic effort will have to be mobilized as soon as possible to take that agenda forward. By 1992 the aim should be for at least twenty universities and comparable institutions worldwide to have set up multidisciplinary programmes—covering moral philosophy, political science, the natural sciences, psychology, jurisprudence and economics—to develop the new conceptual and moral basis for economic life and thought in the 21st century.

Meanwhile, work is needed on specific conceptual aspects of an enabling and conserving economy. Among others, these will include the nature of wealth creation and capital accumulation, and of benefits and costs; the best ways of measuring economic progress, efficiency and productivity; the economic meanings of dependence, self-reliance and interdependence; the economic roles of co-operation and competition; the nature of needs and wants, and the meaning and causes of scarcity; and the meaning of risk and security, together with ways of assessing them and dealing with them.

Remodelling the Structure—Chapters 4 to 8

There are three main tasks here for the early 1990s.

The first task is to develop and spread the idea of the 21st-century economy as an enabling and conserving, multi-level one-world economy, consisting of autonomous but interdependent component parts. These include persons and households, local economies, national economies (and supra-national groupings such as the European Community), the global economy, and the organizations (such as business companies) that carry out economic activities. They and the relationships between them must constitute a system in which one of the main functions of each larger unit will be to enable the smaller units within it to be more self-reliant and conserving. We should aim to have these ideas more fully developed, more generally understood, and more widely accepted by 1992.

The second task is to spread understanding of the idea that this new economic system must and can be evolved by deliberate design as a collective endeavour on the part of humanity as a whole. Again the aim should be to have this idea widely understood and accepted by 1992.

The third task is to begin to tackle the changes needed in each of the component parts, on the lines of the following paragraphs.

Persons and Households

Well before 1992 substantial programmes of public debate, supportive research and practical action should be in hand to foster greater economic self-reliance and more conserving lifestyles at the personal and household level. These should have two main aims. First, they should aim to enlarge people's freedom to act as moral agents in their economic lives, including their opportunities to exercise social and environmental choices in their roles as workers, consumers and savers. Second, they should aim to enlarge the economic role and status of the household and informal sectors of the economy. By 1992 they should have brought firmly on to the mainstream political agenda the need for new approaches to the distribution of incomes and capital.

Local Economies

By 1992 a worldwide homegrown economy movement for self-reliant local development, based on a network of pressure groups and research centres within many countries, should have come into existence. By that date there should be wide and general understanding of the need and potential for local financial institutions, of the socio-economic nature of local economies, of the economic role of local government (including local government taxation, expenditure and finance), and of the enabling function of national government and its public expenditure programmes in relation to self-reliant local development.

National Economies

By 1992 a worldwide network of research centres, pressure groups and individual people—in Western industrialized countries, Third World countries and socialist countries—should have come into existence to promote more self-reliant, more enabling and more conserving national economic policies (and supra-national economic policies in cases such as the European Community). By that date a number of detailed studies on the practical implications of a shift in this direction—of the kinds suggested in Chapter 6—should have been completed and published.

International Economy

As we have seen, our sights should be set on 1992 and 1994/1995—the anniversaries of Columbus and Bretton Woods. Up to 1992 a top priority will be to set in train an international programme of research, discussion and debate on the need to restructure the international economy. Particular emphasis must be given to achieving an enabling and conserving resolution of the Third World debt crisis, and on using the ongoing controversies about the European Single Market and the European Monetary System to research and argue the merits of multi-level currencies and monetary institutions—local, national and international. In 1992 itself, a worldwide reappraisal of the present world economic order will be called for. Thereafter, the immediate aim must be to prepare authoritative proposals for transforming the I.M.F. and World Bank by the end of the century into enabling and conserving economic institutions for a one-world economy, and to launch these proposals in a series of publications, conferences and other events in 1994 and 1995.

Corporate Economy

The aim must be to get it widely understood by 1992—in industrialized, Third World and socialist countries alike, and by both lay people and managers and professionals in business and other organizations of all kinds—that a restructured corporate economy and a more humane and ecological corporate culture will be essential features of an enabling and conserving economic order for the 21st century. By 1992 a number of think-tank/pressure groups should have been established—some at existing business schools, polytechnics or universities—as focal points for programmes of corporate restructuring and corporate cultural change. Also by 1992, phased programmes should have been drawn up for the further development of the co-operative movement, the community business movement, and employee share ownership. These must become mainstream components of the 21st-century economy—which should incorporate the best features of both capitalist and socialist organization but go beyond both.

Redeeming the Money System—Chapters 9 to 12

Fundamental reform of the money system—locally, nationally and internationally—and of people's understanding of it, will be a crucial part of the transition to an enabling and conserving economy. It may be the most challenging part, too. More than almost any other, it will involve getting possibilities on to the agenda for serious discussion and study which are not now regarded as practical. The genuine conceptual difficulties of the issues will be compounded by ingrown institutional mystique. Opening up the money system to constructive critical analysis is bound to be seen by some powerful people as a threat to the source of their power. Some existing financial professionals will resist it as an incursion into their specialist preserves. In some important places, like the Bank of England, the N.I.H. or "not invented here" syndrome may cause knee-jerk resistance against whatever proposals are put forward.

A top priority for the early 1990s must be to achieve widespread understanding of all this. By 1992 it should have become generally accepted that the way today's money system operates is inherently disabling for people, wasteful of resources and destructive of the environment; that the proper functions of money in an enabling and conserving economy are to enable people to transact with one another and to encourage them to act conservingly; that the money system we now have has not been designed to perform these functions efficiently and fairly; that, in redesigning it, we shall find it helpful to understand it and model it both as an information system—an accounting and scoring system—and as a system of flows; and that systems of this kind can be and need to be properly designed to carry out their intended functions.

Between now and 1992 the Third World debt crisis and European monetary developments will be among the issues that can help to bring these more fundamental questions to the fore. But the fundamental questions will need to be pursued in their own right, comprehensively and systematically, in much greater depth than has been possible in Chapters 9 to 12. We should aim to have had in-depth research published on them, and to have initiated widespread discussion of its findings, before the end of 1992.

Taxes

By 1992, specific proposals should have been worked out, and perhaps even to some extent put into practice, to shift the emphasis in taxation as proposed in Chapter 10. Again, widespread understanding is needed that existing tax systems are neither enabling nor conserving. They have not been designed to encourage people to be economically productive or socially useful or to use resources efficiently. The tax burden needs to be shifted from useful human work to the occupation of land and the use of resources that would otherwise have been available for other people. The tax bias against the household economy and informal economic activity needs to be removed. The taxation system—international, national and local—now needs to be understood as a whole. Among its functions at international and national levels should be to encourage national and local economic self-reliance and to redistribute resources between richer and poorer nations and richer and poorer localities. In support of a campaign to raise public awareness on these tax questions, we should aim to have had proper feasibility studies carried out and published by 1992 on combined national and local taxation of the unimproved value of land; national taxation of energy at source; international taxes on imports and currency transfers, and on the extraction of global resources; and pollution taxes at every level—international, national and local.

Incomes and Capital

Another particular priority for the early 1990s is to spread understanding of the need for new approaches to the distribution of incomes and capital. Groups like the Basic Incomes Research Group (BIRG) and the Basic Income European Network (BIEN) must be helped to pursue their studies of how to finance a full Basic Income Scheme which will effectively decouple the right to a living income from dependency either on paid employment or on the dole. This will need to be linked with removing taxes on incomes, and with measures to redistribute capital more widely. The aim should be to have authoritative studies completed and published by 1992. They should contain scenarios exploring the possible economic consequences of the various options, including the likely effects on people's economic behaviour. Separate but linked studies should also be carried out, as proposed in Chapter 11, bringing together in a non-party-political context the scope for wider capital ownership in all its forms, financial and non-financial. Wider capital ownership will help to enable more people to secure a livelihood for themselves without having to be dependent either on paid employment or on the dole.

Currencies, Interest and Debt

By 1992 the aim should be to have made good progress on clarifying the conceptual and theoretical possibilities of a multi-level world currency system, with international, national and local currencies for use in international, national and local transactions; the use of commercial and other non-governmental currencies and quasi-currencies to facilitate economic exchange; and interest-free lending and borrowing. There are prima facie arguments in support of these innovations. But studies are needed on how they might actually be expected to work, how they might be expected to interact with one another, and what their effects on economic behaviour and economic policy-making might actually be. It will also be necessary to look carefully at who will suffer from a conversion of today's monetary and financial system into one that is interest-free, and at what could be done to ease the transition for them. Meanwhile, also before 1992, practical experiments should be encouraged, for example with local currencies and quasi-currencies.

Financial Services and Financial Institutions

Changes outlined in almost every chapter imply changes in today's financial services and financial institutions. All in all, the transition to a new economic order will necessarily bring with it a profound restructuring of this sector of the economy. In this area, like so many discussed in Chapter 13, the conversion of today's way of doing things to the new way will need effective strategic planning. To some extent, it can be left to the pressure of changing market forces to stimulate this. In due course, as the possibility begins to sink in that the prospect of having to move to an enabling and conserving economy may actually be for real, working out conversion strategies for financial institutions will become big business for management consultants and business centres. In the mean time, however, authoritative outside studies—pulling together how the transition to an enabling and conserving economy is likely to affect financial services and financial institutions—need to be carried out and their results published by 1992.

Financial Crash or Soft Landing

The last, but by no means least, of the priority subjects for clarification and research in the monetary and financial area in the next few years will be how to avert or cope with a catastrophic financial collapse. This is a task which government monetary authorities and commercial financial institutions are unlikely to be willing to take on, in case the knowledge that they were doing so might trigger the very thing feared. It is a task for independent outsiders. It will be a difficult one. Chapter 12 has suggested that, even if a world financial collapse would not otherwise have taken place in the 1990s, the need to change direction to an enabling and conserving path of economic development is itself likely to bring one on, unless very effective precautionary measures can be taken. By 1992, assuming a collapse has not already happened by then, the aim should be to be clearer about the possible eventualities that might trigger one, the possible ways of averting one, the possible consequences of one if it happens, and possible responses to those consequences.

Reorientating the Real Economy—Chapter 13

By 1992 the aim should be to have developed and disseminated clear ideas about what an enabling and conserving future path of development will mean for many different aspects of the real economy and real life—work, technology, energy, agriculture, and so on—and what needs to be done to bring about a change of direction to that new path.

This will involve continuing to raise public awareness about possible futures in these various fields in the broader context of an enabling and conserving economy.

It will also involve in-depth preparation of phased programmes of change through the 1990s in all these fields. The aim should be to get programmes published for as many of them as possible by 1992. The great bulk of the activity required to achieve this will fall to people and organizations with a special interest in each of the particular fields in question. But new economics people who understand how the principles of an enabling and conserving economy can be applied across all these different fields, will also have a valuable contribution to make.

The Prospects for Success

These projections all add up to very rapid progress across a very wide front. It is impossible to say at this stage how realistic they are. My previous direct involvement in historic change on this scale—the effective ending of the British Empire some twenty-five to thirty years ago—taught me that, although change tends to come too slowly for those who have seen the need for it, it tends to snowball much faster—once it starts—than has seemed remotely possible to those who haven't.

The extraordinarily rapid rise of environmental awareness in the last two or three years is a sign of hope. Once enough people see that we need a new economics for people as well as for the Earth, and that the two go inextricably together, great progress will be possible in quite a short space of time. I hope this book will help to stimulate many who have not already done so, to work out for themselves how the principles "enable and conserve" can be applied to their own particular field of endeavour.

In trying to clarify the new economic agenda for the 1990s, as I have tried to do, it is difficult to avoid a conflict of moods—a tension between optimism and pessimism.

On the one hand, there is an inescapable sense of exhilaration and high aspiration. Making the transition to a new economic order is perhaps the most crucial challenge to action and thought which faces the world today. If humankind can meet this challenge, a new era will open up for much more than just the economic side of life. It is inspiring just to be among those who are working at this new frontier of history.

Against this it is sometimes hard to shake off an almost desperate sense of inadequacy. As a writer, I am all too conscious of how difficult it is to present a clear picture of what kind of process the transition to a new economic order will be; of all the different types of activity—including the activities of research and reconceptualization—which it will involve; of how all these must cross-link and support one another; of which activities are to do with achieving changes directly now and which to do with getting the possibility of more far-reaching changes on to the mainstream agenda; and of how the very many different kinds of people involved can support one another's efforts. As a former director of research into economic and social and technical change, I sometimes think how much could be done to clarify and take forward the urgent key questions, if only one had a budget of half a million pounds a year—peanuts compared with the billions now being spent in all sorts of other ways. And then I reflect that, even with five times that backing, one could only make a small contribution to the great tide of thought and action that has to be generated worldwide.

This great gap between the scale of the task we face and the capacity of each one of us facing it, reflects the nature of the challenge. I cannot now foresee, and nor can any reader or user of this book, how or with what success the kind of programme it proposes will be realized through the 1990s. My hope can only be that, with all its weaknesses and omissions, the book will give some help to some people in their efforts to move things in the right direction; that the whole process will snowball; and that in three or four years' time it will prove necessary and possible to rewrite the book accordingly, or at least to fill out its practical conclusions and bring them up to date.

Appendix

The New Economics Movement

Some Additional Notes

The notes and references following each chapter, together with the text itself, will have conveyed some idea of what the new economics movement is about and what ground it covers. Many of the books mentioned, including *The Sane Alternative*, *Future Work*, and *The Living Economy* contain many further useful references. This Appendix lists a few additions which readers may find helpful. It is subjective, as well as very incomplete. It could hardly be otherwise. The movement is not sharply defined. Different people come to it from different backgrounds and standpoints. We take part in it in different ways and different places. We each see only part of the picture.

I came to it—though I wasn't then aware of a new economics movement as such—in 1974 when *The Sunday Times* published an article of mine on "Can We Have A Non-Profit Economy?". I was then fascinated by the need for institutional reform in government, business and finance, and by the interplay between the evolution of ideas on the one hand and economic and social and political change on the other.

The response to that article was one of the factors that led me, within the next year or two, to see that the need for institutional reform in Britain was only one, comparatively minor aspect of a much larger challenge facing humankind as a whole. The stimulus came from a number of different directions. Peter Cadogan, a leading figure in the humanist movement, and Colin Hutchinson, then chairman of the Conservation Society, were among those who joined Alison Pritchard and myself in setting up the *Turning Point* network. Ivan Illich's books offered exciting insights into the dependency-creating tendency of modern development. The writings of Daniel Bell, Herman Kahn and Alvin Toffler provoked the thought that there surely must be other possibilities than the expert-dominated, technology-led, superindustrial future they were heralding. Arthur Koestler's book *The Act of Creation* prompted ideas about the role of creativity in economic and social change. I began to sense that the confluence of a number of different movements was setting the scene for a creative breakthrough in human affairs. Futurism, environmentalism, decentralism, feminism and Third World development were among the most prominent of these. It was in that context that the writings of economists like E.F. Schumacher, E.J. Mishan, Herman Daly and Samuel Brittan, seemed interesting and important.

Thereafter, two dates stand out in my mind.

First, in 1976 Alison Pritchard and I spent ten weeks travelling in the United States and Canada. Our meetings with Hazel Henderson, then at her Princeton Center for Alternative Futures, and with Bill Dyson, then Director of the Vanier Institute of the Family in Ottawa, brought us into contact with many new people. From then on we knew we were part of an international movement.

Second, in 1984 we helped to bring together the group which organized The Other Economic Summit (TOES) in London in June that year. Among others, the group included Jonathon Porritt, Paul Ekins, John Elkington and Duncan Smith from the green or environmentalist movement; Pat Saunders from the Quaker side of the world development movement; and John Davis, George McRobie and Diana Schumacher from the Schumacher tradition—appropriate technology, small is beautiful, and economics as if people mattered. From the beginning TOES has been international in character. TOES meetings have been held in subsequent years in Bonn, Tokyo, Toronto and Paris. Its launching in 1984, followed by the New Economics Foundation in 1986, was a landmark in the development of the new economics movement. *The Living Economy* and the New Economics Foundation's newsletter and other publications are required reading for anyone who wants to know what the new economics movement is about.

Against that background, the following additional references may be helpful. I have limited them to a handful of useful introductory books not already mentioned in the text, and to a few organizations and networks that are set up to deal with enquiries. Besides many other valuable books and publications, there are countless other people and groups in many countries who are actively involved in the new economics. I think, for example, of all the authors of papers summarized in *The Living Economy*; of people involved in TOES in Japan in 1986, like Professors Hisashi Nakamura, Ui Jun, and Sekio Sugioka, Dr Takashi Iwami and Mr Kunihiro Morita; and of many grass-roots movements and small alternative development centres in Asia, Africa and Latin America. But I think that, with this Appendix, readers will have enough additional information to find their way to whatever aspect of the new economics most interests them.

I have listed these additional entries rather arbitrarily under five headings, but most of them overlap this artificial classification.

Alternative Futures

Books

Willis W. Harman, *An Incomplete Guide to the Future*, Norton, 1979.

Hazel Henderson, *Creating Alternative Futures: The End of Economics*, Berkley Windhover, NY, 1978; and *The Politics of the Solar Age: Alternatives to Economics*, Anchor/Doubleday, NY, 1981.

Ronald Higgins, *The Seventh Enemy*, Hodder and Stoughton, 1981.

Ziauddin Sardar, *Islamic Futures: The Shape of Ideas to Come*, Mansell, 1985.

Robert Theobald, *The Rapids of Change: Social Entrepreneurship in Turbulent Times*, Knowledge Systems Inc. (7777 W. Morris Street, Indianapolis, Indiana, USA), 1987.

Publications

Future Survey, ed. Michael Marien, monthly from World Future Society (4916 St. Elmo Ave, Bethesda, MD 20814–5089, USA).

New Options, ed. Mark Satin, monthly from New Options Inc. (PO Box 19324, Washington DC 20036, USA).

Organizations and Networks

Action Linkage (Ann Weiser), 5825 Telegraph Avenue No. 45, Oakland, CA 94609, USA.

The Alternative Future Project, Alternativ Framtid, Hausmannsgt. 27, N–0182 Oslo 1, Norway.

Secretariat For Futures Studies, Hagagatan 23 A 3 tr, S-113 47 Stockholm, Sweden.

TRANET (William Ellis), Box 567, Rangeley, ME 04970, USA.

World Futures Studies Federation (Jim Dator), University of Hawaii, Social Science Research Institute Porteus 720, 2424 Maile Way, Honolulu, Hawaii 96822, USA.

Third World Development

Publications

IDOC Internazionale, every two months from the International Documentation and Communication Centre, via Santa Maria dell 'Anima 30, 00186 Rome, Italy.

New Internationalist, monthly from 42 Hythe Bridge Street, Oxford OX1 2EP.

Organizations and Networks

Association Mondiale de Prospective Sociale (AMPS), CP 56, CH-1211 Geneva 19, Switzerland.

Centre International de Recherche sur l'Environnement et le Developpement (CIRED), 54 Bd Raspail, 75270 Paris, France.

Dag Hammarskjold Foundation, Ovre Slottsgatan 2, S-752 20 Uppsala, Sweden.

International Foundation for Development Alternatives (IFDA), 2 Place du Marche, CH-1260 Nyon, Switzerland.

Pan-African Social Prospects Centre, BP 1501 Porto-Novo, Benin.

Society for International Development (SID), Palazzo Civilta del Lavoro, 00144 Rome, Italy.

Third World Network, 87 Cantonment Road, 10250 Penang, Malaysia.

Sustainable Development

Books

Jonathon Porritt, *Seeing Green*, Basil Blackwell, 1984; and, with David Winner, *The Coming of the Greens*, Fontana, 1988.

Organizations and Networks

U.K. Centre for Economic and Environmental Development (UK CEED) (Director, David Cope), 12 Upper Belgrave Street, London, SW1X 8BA—issues a bi-monthly newsletter.

Worldwatch Institute (President, Lester Brown), 1776 Massachusetts Avenue NW, Washington DC 20036, USA—issues an annual State of the World Report and Worldwatch Papers on aspects of sustainable development.

Small is Beautiful

Books

Romesh Diwan and Mark Lutz (eds.), *Essays in Gandhian Economics*, Gandhi Peace Foundation, 221–223 Deen Dayal Upadhyaya Marg, New Delhi 110002, India.

George McRobie, *Small Is Possible*, Cape, 1981.

E.F. Schumacher, *Small Is Beautiful*, Abacus, 1974; and *Good Work*, Cape, 1979.

Organizations and Networks

Agence de Liaison pour le Developpement d'une Economie Alternative (ALDEA), 28 Bd de Sebastopol, 75004 Paris, France.

Lokayan, 13 Alipur Road, Delhi 110054, India.

Rocky Mountain Institute, Box 505, Snowmass, CO 81654, USA.

Rodale Institute, 222 Main Street, Emmaus, PA 18049, USA.

Sarvodaya International Development Institute, 98 Rawatawattwe Road, Moratuwa, Sri Lanka.

New Economics

Books

Soren Bergstrom (ed.), *Economic Growth and the Role of Science*, Department of Business Administration, Stockholm University, S-106 91 Stockholm, Sweden 1984.

Herman E. Daly, *Steady State Economics*, Freeman, San Francisco 1977.

Joseph Huber, *Die Regenbogen-Gesellschaft: Okologie und Sozialpolitik*, Fischer, Frankfurt, 1985.

Manfred A. Max-Neef, *From the Outside Looking In: Experiences in Barefoot Economics*, Dag Hammarskjold Foundation, Uppsala, 1982.

Bootstrap Press (Suite 9A, 777 United Nations Plaza, New York NY10017, USA) is an imprint of the Intermediate Technology Development Group/North America (Chairman, Ward Morehouse). It publishes a series of new economics books including:

David P. Ross and Peter J. Usher, *From the Roots Up: Economic Development as if Community Mattered*, 1986.

George Benello, Robert Swann and Shann Turnbull, *Building Sustainable Communities: Tools and Concepts for Self-Reliant Economic Change*, 1989.

Organizations and Networks

Centre for the Study of Urban, Rural and Development Alternatives (CEPAUR), Casilla 95, Correo Miramontes, Santiago, Chile.

Council on Economic Priorities, 30 Irving Place, New York, NY 10003, USA.

European Centre for Work and Society, PO Box 3073, 6202 NB Maastricht, Holland.

Human Economy Center, Box 14, Economics Department, Mankato State University, Mankato, MN 56001, USA.

Living Economy Network (Co-ordinator, Paul Ekins), School of Peace Studies, University of Bradford, Bradford, West Yorkshire BD7 1DP.

The Other Economic Summit/North America (TOES/NA) (Communications Co-ordinator, Susan Hunt), Economics Department, University of Maine, Orono, ME 04469, USA.

Index

The index includes references to subjects, authors, publications and organizations discussed in the text, but the notes at the end of the chapters have not been indexed. References have been arranged in word-by-word alphabetical order.
Elizabeth Wiggans